```
**************************************************************
*                                                            *
*                                                            *
*    LEGAL ASPECTS:   ACQUIRING AND PROTECTING SOFTWARE      *
*                                                            *
*------------------------------------------------------------*
*                                                            *
*               By:   Bruce K. Brickman, Esq.                *
*                                                            *
*                                                            *
**************************************************************
```

Carnegie Press, Inc.
100 Kings Road
Madison, New Jersey
(201) 822-1240

To my wife Judy, whose support,
encouragement and keen insights
made this book possible.

ACKNOWLEDGEMENTS

This book could not have been written without the cooperation of a number of people for whose assistance the author is deeply grateful. I extend my sincere thanks to George O'Connor, Thursten Clarke, Michael A. Daniels, Esq., Leonard F. Turi, Frank Kemp, James Dowd, Stephen Kahn, Esq., and Jack Berger.

The nature of the contributions of these fine people was dictated by their own individual professions and disciplines. I thoroughly enjoyed working with each one of them and hope, somehow, that the feeling was mutual.

BRUCE K. BRICKMAN

ABOUT THE AUTHOR

Bruce K. Brickman, Esq., is a nationally recognized expert in high technology law. He has an in-depth understanding of the computer, telecommunications and robotics industries. With his knowledge of the Uniform Commerical Code and proprietary devices for protecting intellectual property (copyright and trade secret), he is able to structure the legal support necessary for buying, using, accessing, leasing, owning and protecting technology.

Mr. Brickman has been featured as a keynote speaker by numerous trade associations, institutions, business and professional groups. He regularly provides public seminars on behalf of the American Institute for Professional Education, as well as private seminars for Fortune 500 corporations.

Mr. Brickman is the author of "Solving The Computer Contract Dilemma," and "How to Negotiate a Big Ticket Contract." He is currently counsel to the law firms of Braverman & Rosen (New York City) and Rosen, Szegda and Gersowitz (Hackensack, N.J.).

TABLE OF CONTENTS

CHAPTER I

NATURE AND GROWTH OF
THE ELECTRONIC INFORMATION PROCESSING INDUSTRY

People believe that the technology of electronic information processing will solve all problems. This mystique has helped catapult the computer industry from the 1951 sale of the first commerical computer to over a $100-billion-dollar-plus market.

Understanding how this industry grew and developed is critical to dealing with its presence and perceiving its future. Like any technically oriented industry it began with a burst of innovation. New products, manufactured by small organizations founded by engineers were developed to leap the barriers of mechanical number crunching. These products were limited to narrow applications. Operating in isolation, and massive in size, they depended solely on the ever unpredictable and always expensive vacuum tube, but they were the forerunners--and innovation begets innovation. In the late 50's, engineers tinkering with technology created the transistor. Smaller, cheaper, and more powerful than the vacuum tube, it reduced product mass, increased processing speed, and widened the number of applications that could be performed.

Suddenly, commercial success became a function of size and power. Small size reduced production costs, while greater power meant broader applications resulting in multi-task products

1

(those that could operate more than one type of application, such as word processing and number crunching). As functionality broadened and products proliferated, the typical end user at that time was confronted by the potential chaos of unrestrained information flow. (Remember that at this stage, although its size had shrunk, the average computer was still the size of a walk-in closet, requiring air conditioning and special flooring. The market, though widened, was limited to major corporations and institutions that could afford the significant investment of dollars needed to acquire and maintain those products.) The information flow was so massive and uncontrolled, it threatened to swamp the user with its own data. To solve this problem, data centers were established to consolidate processing operations and create systems to manage information flow. Although products were still limited in functionality (for example, applications like word processing were performed on machines dedicated solely to that operation), at least output was centralized so that management could control distribution. The advent of the "data center" altered corporate structure by instituting an internal power base that could control traditional management functions simply by setting priorities for data processing and limiting distribution of output.

By the late 60's the proverbial bright engineers with unlimited vision and enormous energy, were searching for the technological answer that would unlock electronic information processing to the world, not just to the Fortune 500. The answer was found in the micro chip. Now, just a thin silicon wafer was all that was necessary to house the circuitry previously found in machines the size of a living room. The revolution had begun. As the transistor shrank, the micro chip shriveled, and the world teetered at the edge of the possible. An industry blossomed with new, powerful, and more affordable products. Innovation was measured in months, sometimes weeks, and ideas were transformed into reality at a dizzying pace. The seventies became a time of engineers with ideas, creating products that "took-off," resulting in multi-million dollar markets. Classic, is the Apple Computer, which rode a $1500 investment in the first personal computer to become a corporate giant in less than three years. Simultaneously, users were beginning to flex their collective economic muscles, taking over the direction of new product development by dictating market needs. Driven by large users, demand increased for more powerful systems with wider applications. This created an entire industry dedicated to combining hardware and software to produce turnkey systems "customized" to the needs of such data centers. As powerful systems were developed, users pressured vendors to provide point of sale support by distributing information to remote locations for processing. Industries such as insurance, securities and consumer retail goods wanted sales representatives to have the flexibility of "calling up" live data from a host computer for the purpose of changing client accounts or obtaining potential gross margin to close new sales. This demand changed the function of the consolidate data center from information management to distribution processing, creating a market for products that could enhance the speed and power of interactive processing (communication between machines). With the birth of the small and affordable personal computer, the dream of universal access had become a possiblity. The market for electronic information processing products was both rich and virtually limitless, attracting not only start-up vendors but cross-overs from other product areas--for instance, Coleco jumped from toys to video games and then to computers. As competition intensified, particularly in the personal computer product area, single-product organizations, managed primarily by engineers, failed to respond effectively by broadening market base. This resulted in a shake-out producing bankruptcies like that of Osborne Computer. Even giants like Texas Instruments misjudged opportunities. After selling more than two million micro computers, it was compelled by more aggressive competition to withdraw from that market.

Concurrent with the initial shakeout was the paradox of an industry growing flaccid. While vendors proliferated and new sub-industries (for example, computer security) sprang up, many of the once lean, small entrepreneurial organizations became less interested in pursuing technology and more concerned with quick turnover. Financial managers took over from the founding engineers. Small enterprises, grown fat with market success, added layers of middle management, slowing the development of technology. Innovation became mired in bureaucracy.

To rekindle the initial zest of discovery, companies began spinning off work groups, "companies within companies" (IBM has 14), permitting engineers to pursue technological goals unhampered by organizational constraints. Such groups were often set up secretly as separate organizations with little or no control by top management. With money as the motivation, workaholic entrepreneurial drive impelled the creation of state of the art products at rates rivaling those achieved during the '70's. The result: A new surge of technical innovation creating the fourth generation of products with multi-task memories embedded in firmware built into the equipment, reducing size and increasing power.

Focus on Software: The software sector illustrates the data processing industry's growth from cottage to big business.

Software programs govern the computer's processing of information. The two major program types are: operation and application. The operating program directs the flow of data and the application programs accomplish particular tasks. Think of a city as an analogy. Computer hardware is the road system, using circuitry as the paths travelled by electronic commands. The software operating program provides general instructions for directing traffic, as stop lights and yield signs do on the road. The software application program directs how particular tasks are to be performed. Together, the hardware, the software operating program, and the application programs create an integrated and compatible "system" for processing information.

The Beginning: Clearly, software is critical to the performance of data processing functions. Remarkably, however, during the initial stage of data processing industry development, software was considered something of a byproduct and was virtually given away with the equipment. In 1957, IBM signed a consent decree with the Justice Department "unbundling" (agreeing not to provide) software with its computers. This decree marked the real beginning of the software industry, because it created the need for independent suppliers.

The Development: Those who started producing software incurred none of the overhead that confronted hardware manufacturers. Access to a computer, an idea, talent, and energy were all that was required to become a software manufacturer. Such low entrance barriers attracted an influx of engineers--many of them graduates of IBM--who focused on software for particular applications. As machines became more powerful and affordable, users demanded sophisticated software products capable of handling numerous functions at ever increasing speeds. The

6

profit margin was relatively high, since the same product could be licensed to multiple users increasing the magnitude of each unit's mark-up. Indeed, vendors would finance research by contracting with a user to develop, at the user's expense, a new product to be owned and marketed by the particular software house. This resulted in expensive high margin products created at no cost to the vendor. The dynamics of a fast paced, lucrative software market attracted management professionals interested in packaging and distributing a variety of software products. One of the key developments in the late 60's and early 70's was the appearance of distribution houses which licensed marketing rights from program authors and then used promotional techniques to create national markets for those products. For example, Visicalc was originally developed by Software Arts. Its distribution right was sold to Visicorp, which created a market demand resulting in sales of over 600,000 copies. The software industry, however, was still very much cottage oriented. Engineers would create particular products and license them to distribution organizations that would concentrate promotion in technical journals aimed at business organizations with expensive computer installations. This rapid development of faster, more powerful microcomputers changed this dependence on cottage developers by creating demand for more versatile products. Previously, software programs were designed for single applications such as word processing, graphics or spreadsheet (number crunching); however, driven by more sophisticated machines, broader applications, combining multiple functions (such as those indicated above), were possible. The development of such multi-task application products in the short time period allotted by competition requires money, professional management, and promotion. The Lotus Development Company was one of the first to meet all the requirements of market demand. Backed by $5 million dollars in venture capital and using $1 million to finance a promotional campaign for the Lotus 1,2,3 product, it created a tremendous demand for a microcomputer product that had several major applications: word processing, graphics and spreadsheet. The market responded with distributers and software development companies producing multi-task products, expanding the demand for inexpensive but powerful software designed to operate on micro-computers. Sales grew from 20.6%, from $5.5 billion in 1980 to $11.7 billion by 1984. This growth attracted major corporations from other industries, which began acquiring software distributers or development companies. For instance, McKesson Corporation--a Fortune 500 Company involved in the distribution of drugs and health care items--acquired SKU, Inc., a national distributer of programs for personal computers. Software had now become a professionally-managed, well-financed industry. No longer could a lone entrepreneur develop a product, place an ad in Byte Magazine, and be assured of sales. It now takes tremendous financial backing to elbow out the competition and carve a niche in a fast-moving, dynamic market.

The Legal Swamp: Strong financing is needed, however, not only to maintain a competitive edge but to finance sky-rocketing litigation costs. It is conservatively estimated that lawsuits occur in one out of every ten transactions involving the acquisition or use of electronic data processing products or services. Users have discovered that litigation is an effective way of using poor product performance. Software vendors, in particular OEMs providing turnkey systems and emphasizing product customization to fit a user's specific needs, are generally more likely than others to be subject to litigation. Such litigation usually results from misunderstanding caused by overly high expectations on the part of the user (shades of computer mystique). Responding to the threat of consequential damages, software houses have increased their emphasis on "canned" (non-customized) software programs, and OEMs have often refused major customization of systems. In addition, the emphasis has shifted from the earlier reliance on end-user financing of new product development to the use of venture capital, R&D tax shelters, and acquisitions. Finally, vendors have employed sophisticated contracts designed to insulate themselves from liability without encroaching on product promotion.

As a result, a vendor must do more than field a software product that provides a technological edge, and amass millions of dollars to finance promotion and professional management. To continue research and development, he requires the involvement of parties outside the industry such as venture capitalists or acquisition hungry corporations. The nature of such third party financing is examined by Michael A. Daniels, Esq., an attorney with considerable experience in that area, in an article titled "Financing High Technology Growth Situations" that follows this paragraph. Mr. Daniels discusses the type of financing arrangement most often used by high tech vendors, how those arrangements work, and who is involved in them.

FINANCING HIGH TECHNOLOGY GROWTH SITUATIONS

The emergence since the end of World War II of technology-based growth industries will be pondered by historians for many years to come. Are we living in a "technological era," a "technological society," or a "technological system"? Which is the major business trend of our time? Evidence mounts that the extent of technology-driven business opportunities is multiplying and that business people who have taken advantage of this situation are winning more and more of the business battles. This technology push requires many key elements in order to successfully translate research and development from laboratories into successful business products. What is most striking about the current time is that more and more U.S. and foreign based investors, business people and professionals in all pursuits are betting hard money on the potential payoffs of new technology.

In order for technology of any type to reach commercially viable take-off levels, financing of some type is required. Without the money to back the concepts, prototypes and designs of the technicians, the technology will never see the light of the marketplace. In this article we will review the use of the most common financial mechanisms in promoting the technologies headed for the market place of the world.

The review will include the use of venture capital, private investors, R&D Limited Partnerships, corporate funding programs, and mergers and acquisitions as financing catalysts to industry growth. Additionally, we will comment on the usual small-scale technology situation which begins as a design or prototype, and how this situation is normally developed into a business plan suitable for potential financing. Finally, a look at the current public offering of stock from a technology venture will be reviewed and analyzed as a major financing mechanism for selected technology concepts with the "right investor" appeal.

A.   THE SMALL-SCALE R & D SITUATION

No small-scale research and development situation is "typical," since we will always find variations in the scenarios, revolving principally around the individuals involved (the people-side) and the technology concept (the product- or service side). Given that no situation is "typical," there are certain characteristics that do tend to appear in most of these small start-up, concept-stage situations. The characteristics commonly found are:

-- Little capital.

-- Little knowledge on the part of the technical personnel involved as to what to do now from a business standpoint.

-- Lack of contacts into marketing, business and financial circles.

Many situations involving new technology concepts contain these common elements. There is generally a strong sense of individual ownership at stake, and an atmosphere of suspicion of outsiders who might attempt to pirate the idea, concept or prototype away from the founder or inventor. An air of mistrust is usually found when any outsider enters the picture. If you do not understand and act accordingly in these situations from the first meeting, your chances of resolving this mistrust and moving forward in a positive and mutually beneficial mode are very low. Personalities are key block points in technology areas, as inventors and small business founders with good and potentially valuable ideas are "loners" by most measures. Successful business people deal in this emerging growth environment by understanding the personal feelings of the founders and inventors and being able to explain the advantages of moving a concept, design or prototype along to commercial marketability status. This process is usually a longer and more arduous task than originally envisioned. Financing and nurturing the small-scale R&D situation to the point of market viability is not a task for those who have a low tolerance or persistance level. Persistance, directness and confidence-building are paramount to successful progress with these types of ventures.

It is estimated that most of the new technology advances are eminating from the small R&D based firms, garages, and workbenches of entrepreneurial technicians. Given the complexity of the rapid technology advances now underway, it is impossible to prove conclusively that this is in fact the case. Technological innovation comes from many sources, both large and small. The point is, for most of you, a small-scale research and development situation will be part of your activity at some point. You will meet the founders and inventors of the next great widget at a trade show, a high technology seminar, through your attorney, banker or accountant, or through ads in the local newspaper. The significance of understanding this situation is that when you do face that founder or inventor, you must be able to separate the wheat from the chaff as quickly and expeditiously as possible. If you do not learn to separate the good ones from the time-wasters (their own and yours) you will be involved in long, non-productive periods. Most keen observers of inventors and founders look for fierce determination, a practical concept that can be developed fairly rapidly, and something that fits into the marketplace which is already in place or is emerging. The one-in-a-thousand long-shot is just that--a long-shot.

B. PRIVATE INVESTORS

As used in this section, "private investors" means friends, family, and individuals who invest in small-scale emerging technology investment areas. Most new start-up firms receive their initial capital from the founders, the founders' friends, relatives or colleagues. As the firm progresses, lines of credit are usually obtained at local banks; houses and cars are signed over to banks as collateral to secure the loans for the company; and the entrepreneurs go to work. For those firms that survive the first three- to five-year make-it-or-break-it period typical of small business start-ups, there emerges a need for additional financing in order to move forward into the technology battle. It is at this point that consideration begins to be given to outside sources of funding. Typically, the founders will attempt to place more of their own money into the business for product or service development, or go again to friends and relatives for loans or in exchange for stock. When these sources are exhausted, the search for other private sources of funding widens. Usually, the owners and founders prefer to find a single or several private individuals who like to invest in new growth technology firms and have done so in the past. These people are usually located by word-of-mouth or by small ads in newspapers. Doctors, lawyers, businessmen, accountants and other professionals are the usual source for these types of funds. My experience indicates, as a rule of thumb, that local professionals are the source for perhaps 75% of the funding, immediately after friends and relatives. As interest in funding technology-based firms has risen, clubs, forums, and groups have formed, in most major U.S. cities, which attempt to link investors and technical/businessmen looking for additional funds for corporate growth. We have even reached the point in some technology-oriented areas such as San Francisco, Boston, Chicago, Washington, and Dallas, where major conferences are now held specifically for the purpose of linking investors with firms looking for capital resources. This type of linkage activity will continue to grow in the U.S. in the next five years.

More sophisticated inventors and businessmen with technology products and services have begun to search for financing from sources outside of their immediate areas. Washington, D.C. technical entrepreneurs now routinely travel to New York City and Boston, seeking the right sources for their particular ventures. Traffic between Texas and California has increased dramatically in the past five years in the search for funding for new start-up enterprises. If you are looking for funding, you should bear in mind that private investors are a large source of initial funding in the early years, for most technology-based businesses. You should search your local area carefully for firms and individuals known to have interests as investors in the technology sector. If you are a private investor looking for good investments, your

local area may be as good a place to look as the other
side of the country, and probably a better place to
look, since you can more closely monitor the progress of
the investment in the particular company. The key to
both sides of this private investment coin is to keep
your eyes and ears open for sources. It is amazing how
much you can pick up if you just listen, and focus on
your objective of locating the right match-up for you.

A private investment in the next IBM is obviously the
place that every investor wants to be. This is tough.
It takes knowledge of the industry in order to make a
valid assessment and judgment of a proper investment
candidate. The more knowledgable you become on the
particular place that a new product or service idea
fits, the more likely you are to succeed with your
investment. Do your homework well.

For the business person or technical person looking for
funds, know what you want--exactly--in terms of money,
and be prepared to present a case to the private
investor(s) that clearly states what the funds will be
used for. A presentation full of holes and poorly
thought through will bring you only "no" as an answer.
Prepare and rehearse. You are on stage even though it
is out of character for you. Be honest, and tell the

short-falls as well as the gleaming prospects. Smart
investors know your world well from the business and
market viability side. They want you to prove to them
that you have what the market wants, not what you think
they want to hear.

C.   VENTURE CAPITAL

As the growth of technology-based firms has advanced, we
have been moving rapidly from the small scale research
and development situation previously described and the
private family-and-friends investment scenario into
areas when firms began to advance past the one- or two-
man stage into the realm of financing possibilities at
larger scale levels. This financing picture develops as
a technology concept moves along, and it is time to
begin planning the next level of firm development where
larger scale money is required, more technical talent is
needed, and professional advice is required in several
areas. When firms reach this stage of development,
venture capital becomes one primary option for growth
consideration.

For our purposes, "venture capital" means money flowing
into technology-based areas from more traditional
sources, i.e., venture capital firms, investment banking

sources and newly formed venture capital funds. The key feature in this particular financing area has been the dramatic growth of available venture capital in the past 3-5 year period. It is becoming common knowledge that venture capital is more readily available now than at any time in the past. This appears to be correct. It leads to the conclusion that venture capital will serve as a major source of financing for technology firms in the foreseeable future. It is estimated that in 1975, only $10 million in private capital venture funds was raised in the U.S. In 1981, it is estimated, approximately $1.3 billion was available in venture capital in the U.S. This is staggering growth in the availability of funds and willingness of venture capitalists to invest. In 1983, it is estimated, well over $3 billion in venture capital was available in the U.S. market. This is one financing mechanism that has had a tremendous impact on newly emerging technology companies. This seed capital--on a more professional, larger scale--has spurred the growth of technology-based industries in such fields as telecommunications, medicine, genetics, robotics and computer-aided design and manufacturing.

Venture capital is typically found in venture capital companies, Small Business Investment Companies (SBIC's), and, recently, in brokerage firms, major corporations, and investment banking houses. Success stories in technology industries of small start-up firms that have richly rewarded early investors has obviously served as a major catalyst to push more players into the picture.

There is no doubt that this surge of venture capital seeking a home in primary growth areas of high technology will reshape growth patterns of the entire industry spectrum. As larger capital players enter the funding picture, competition will grow more intense, industry shakeout will occur more rapidly, and realignments for survival will become more commonplace. In a short, ten-year period, the changes in venture capital financing for technology-growth companies has reached a point where it is dramatically affecting the long-term business prospects of hundreds of organizations.

Competition for technology ideas, concepts and viable market entry products is becoming more intense, and will continue to increase. Technology-oriented individuals with something to sell will continue to demand in the future, and there will be no lack of interested investors. It appears that inventors and founders with marketable products and services in technology areas will be able to offer their proposals more easily to an increasing number of venture capital sources. This will enable them to bid up the amount of potential capital to be raised, as well as to drive tougher business in terms of equity control for themselves than has been the case in the recent past. For the short-term, it appears that supply-and-demand is operating in favor of the suppliers of technology. This is the reverse condition of that which existed just a few short years ago. We will see more situations where funds are raised for venture capital purposes in the technology area from foreign investors. The growing gap between European and U.S. technology advances will act as a continuing catalyst for foreign venture capital flow into the U.S. Additionally, as investment flow becomes ever more internationalized, U.S. technology-based investments will become more attractive.

D.   CORPORATE FUNDING PROGRAMS

As corporate America has come to realize, technology innovation and "hot" product developments often emerge from little, obscure, and unknown sources. This realization has led a number of large and medium-sized corporations in the U.S. to set up corporate funding programs that attempt to locate promising venture areas

21

in emerging technologies. These programs take various forms, but have tended to be structured as joint-venture arrangements, venture capital funds that are captives of the corporations, or exclusive rights arrangements for future products developed by the small entity on the cutting edge of a particular technology. This increasing interest on the part of major corporations is emerging technologies and of individuals or firms associated with particular technologies has been a new and dynamic development in the financing area for technology. There is every reason to believe that this source of financing or emerging technologies will grow, as large corporations search feverishly for new technology-growth areas to bolster corporate growth and rates-of-return. The desire of many technical and scientific personnel, and entrepreneurially-oriented executives in the corporate world, to move into less rigid business structures and to make a more risk-oriented approach for potentially greater financial rewards (personnally), will necessitate increased corporate arrangements of this nature. The typical arrangement that has been emerging is for the corporation to provide seed capital and then have rights to manufacture and distribute the resulting technology-based product. In a growing number of instances, the corporation providing the seed capital has a major interest in profiting from the emerging company in a public offering, if the technology is successful. This is then a pure investment view from the corporate standpoint. Look for more foreign corporations to enter into joint ventures and to seed funding arrangements with emerging U.S. based technology growth sector companies, as foreign firms seek to enhance their U.S. market presence in the new technologies.

E.   RESEARCH AND DEVELOPMENT LIMITED PARTNERSHIPS

Since 1981 research and development (R&D) limited partnerships have taken their place alongside other financing mechanisms as viable and useful tools in funding developmental technology products. Changes in the tax law provided for coverage of certain product development. In 1982, Barron's ran an article on R&D tax shelters, calling them the "Hottest Thing in Tax Shelters." The interesting feature of this form of technology financing is that small as well as large organizations can take advantage of the benefits of this mechanism. A small enterprise with potentially marketable scientific concepts can enter this area for funding, as well as large, firmly-established multinationals that may want to share the risk of state-of-the-art technology. In both cases R&D Limited

Partnership may be appropriate for the financing. High tax bracket investors who are willing to risk an investment of this nature and are also looking for potentially significant payoff if a technological breathrough occurs, appear to find this type of financing mechanism particularly attractive as an investment vehicle.

Two common forms of R&D limited partnership have recently emerged. One form, and by far the most common, is an arrangement whereby a new firm or established firm structures R&D project and uses a limited partnership for the individual investors to invest in as limited partners. As in most limited partnerships, this structure is used to allow the investors to take current tax deductions for a large portion of their investment in the R&D limited partnership arrangement. In this case, the partnership contracts with the corporation to undertake the actual research and development of the scientific or technological idea, concept or design. Another form of this arrangement is one whereby two corporations are involved: one is under contract with the other to perform the research and development, and the other, the funding corporation, is allowed to market and distribute the product developed.

Typically, funds for these arrangements have been raised through private placements. This mechanism simply means that the units of the limited partnership have been sold privately, instead of in a public offering of the units in the investment. Bear in mind that although the private placement route is the most common, there has been a gradually increasing number of situations in this area that have been sold publicly. A public sale of these units requires the usual registration with the Securities and Exchange Commission (SEC) while the private placement route is not registered with the SEC. In the private placement situation, the units are offered through a placement memorandum and circulated to a limited number of potential investors. In this private placement situation, the investors would invest their funds in the R&D limited partnership, and the corporation would obtain the funds through that limited partnership to undertake the developmental work on the technology. The corporation normally provides the basic technology as its investment into the R&D limited partnership arrangement, and may either sell or, more typically, license to the partnership the rights to the technology. Obviously, the corporation's interest is best served by retaining access to the technology and having this technology available for future use and development. Bear in mind that details and structuring of these arrangements vary widely in practice.

A few recently reported examples of R&D limited partnership arrangements give a flavor of the current environment. An amount of $3,000,000 was reportedly raised by Philon Partners in twenty; limited partnership interests at $150,000 per unit for research and development incidental to future production of sophisticated computer language compilers. It is reported that $5,407,500 was raised by Bioassay Research Limited Partnership for research and development in biotechnology areas. One of the largest R&D limited partnerships reported to date was in the amount of $55,600,000 raised in a private placement for Genetech Clinical Partners, Ltd. The funds were to be used for clinical development of Human Growth Hormone and Gamma Interferon as human therapeutic products. These three examples illustrate the range of both funds and products that are now being invested under the R&D limited partnership structure. There is every indication that as investor interest grows in both technology development and tax shelter mechanisms, this area will play an increasingly important role in moving technology industries along the growth path.

F.   ACQUISITIONS AND MERGERS

Acquisitions and mergers should always be considered from the viewpoint of financing mechanisms. As the growth and glamour of technology fields have unfolded over the past ten-year period, more and more large and medium sized corporations have been investigating entry into fields they are not involved in through the merger or, more typically, acquisition mechanism. This has resulted in a growing number of acquisitions in every high-technology field. The larger corporate players have been interested in acquiring smaller, promising technology companies, and the small firms have had to grow quickly, merge or be acquired, in order to remain in a competitive position. All rapidly emerging business fields exhibit significant activity in the merger and acquisition areas as rapid technology change and money flow into growth sectors of the economy.

Recent changes in the computer hardware area, specifically in the micro and personal computer fields, are classic examples of this phenomena. There is every indication that merger and acquisition activity will grow, and play a major role in shaping the technology environment through the end of this century. In a recent study by Broadview Associates of New Jersey, it was estimated that more than $1 billion would be spent in 1983 to acquire computer services companies. The study noted that 15 years ago, the total annual revenue of the entire computer service industry was $1 billion and that the figure had now grown to revenue of $26 billion per annum. The study stated that the previous highest annual dollar volume spent on computer services company acquisitions was $756 million in 1981. These figures illustrate the magnitude of the market and the dynamic situation in the merger and acquisition area which has now evolved. Bear in mind that these figures are only for acquisitions in the computer service company areas. The reason that this activity will grow as a financing mechanism as well as a business competition method is that every major domestic and foreign firm is examining how to gain a foothold in this true growth market. As more competitors enter the field, they will find that the quickest entry point is by acquisition of existing technology firms that have a particular market niche and are already actively involved in the market.

Acquisitions usually provide the small technology firm access to larger pools of capital for more rapid and dynamic expansion. They also provide the skilled professional business talent that is a vital ingredient in the growth of the firm over the long-haul. Additionally, the founders of the small technology firms have increased incentives to sell to larger firms, as prices for small technology growth firms have escalated sharply in the past three years. Look for merger and acquisition activity to increase, for larger non-technology firms to move into this area for growth, and for these mechanisms to serve as major components fueling growth in technology fields in the years ahead. Foreign firms have special interest in acquisitions in the American technology marketplace, because they wish to acquire existing firms for market penetration, along with the rights to technologies developed in America and unavailable in their own, foreign, organizations. British, French, West German, and Japanese firms appear to be particularly active in acquisition of U.S.based technology firms. This trend will continue.

G.   PUBLIC OFFERINGS

Technology companies with substantial changes of high growth usually plan to "go public" from start-up, if the opportunity exists. Selling stock of a small company offers the owners and the company substantial capital resources and brings the company and its technology base to both the investor and the business communities.

There are significant advantages in pursuing this financing mechanism. Technology companies, as well as other business concerns seeking to sell stock on the public market, are constrained by the general stock market environment, as well as by having a firm that has wide enough "investor appeal" to sell the stock. Initial or new public offerings of U.S. companies have run in cycles over the past twenty years. The years of 1968-72 were good years for new technology firms to enter the public markets. The year 1969 was a high-water mark until 1983 for new public offerings, with 1969 registering 1,026 initial public offerings and a total of $2,605,000,000 raised in these offerings. For 1983, well over 1,100 new public offerings were undertaken, with more than $15,000,000,000 raised. These 1983 figures include savings and loans and mutual savings banks whose offerings are not registered with the SEC. However measured, 1983 was the year of the new public offering. In the first half of 1983, technology companies were the primary beneficiaries of this new-issue market surge. Billions of dollars were raised for newly emerging high technology firms in a wide range of fields. Particularly active were the new issues in telecommunications, computer hardware and software, medical instrumentation, and computer-aided design and manufacturing. This infusion of capital through the public offering mechanism has had a significant effect on perceptions of founders of high technology firms. Founders now look closely at the option of "going public" with new start-up technology concerns or with established technology companies that have reached the stage of developing products and services with attractive "investor" growth features. A significant development in the past two years in this financing mechanism area has been the entry of large, nationally recognized brokerage firms into the field. Technology companies of recent vintage had a difficult task several years ago getting in the front door of the major brokerage firms. Now the major brokerage houses are actively looking for prime public offering candidates. This is a drastic development that brings major financing participants into the new public offering arena. Following were the ten leading underwriters of new public offerings, excluding thrifts, during the first half of 1983:

Company	Dollars Raised (in millions)
L.F. Rothschild	$798.1
Hambrecht & Quist	$694.2
Alex. Brown & Sons	$490.2
Merrill Lynch	$447.4
Prudential-Bache	$426.9
Shearson/American Express	$383.1
Robertson, Colman	$348.5
Morgan Stanley	$345.0
E.F. Hutton & Co.	$235.2
Dean Witter	$224.5

As indicated above, these ten underwriters raised over $3 billion in the first half of 1983 for new public offering firms. This increasing activity in the new issue area, as well as the number of national and regional brokerage houses that have decided that they need to be actively involved in this financing area, now offer emerging technology firms expanded options in obtaining financing. If market conditions hold fairly steady in the next several years, technology firms will have the opportunity to take advantage of this marketplace. What will develop will be the constant search for the quality new-technology issues out of the many firms seeking to pursue this financing route. Recent examples of technology firms going public in 1983 indicate the range of firms involved and the capital raised during the 1983 period:

COMPANY	SHARES	PRICE	$ RAISED
BIOGEN	2,500,000	$23.00	$57,500,000
GTECH	2,050,000	$13.25	$27,162,500
IOMEGA	2,000,000	$10.00	$20,000,000

The first of these firms, BIOGEN, is involved in genetic engineering fields, the second, GTECH, is a data networking firm and the third, IOMEGA, is in the disc drive field. These examples are typical of the types of firms that sold stock to the public during 1983.

Indicators point to additional capital being placed in the new issue market by a widening variety of investors, ranging from middle-class individuals to foreign companies. As technology growth companies continue to out-perform older more mature industrial sectors the funding available through the new issue market for technology growth companies should continue to be substantial. This particular financing mechanism will fluctuate with the usual ups and downs of the market, but with major national financial institutions now actively involved in this area, you should anticipate that this financing mechanism will offer increasing opportunities for high technology growth firms.(1)

Recommended reading for those interested in the use of

venture capital to finance business enterprises is a booklet by
Deloitte, Haskins and Sells titled <u>Raising Venture Capital</u>. A
section detailing the investment information normally required by
venture capital organizations is reprinted with their permission.

Section 2: The Business Plan Format (from the Deloitte, Haskins & Sells booklet <u>Raising Venture Capital: An Entrepreneur's Guidebook</u>.

Though sharing common requirements, business plans take
many sizes, shapes, and forms. Your plan must describe
the product or service to be sold; the market for that
product or service (whether that market exists or must
be created); how the product will be made or the service
performed; who is involved in the company; how much
money the company needs and what it will do with it;
and, most important, how the investors will make a
return on their money and when they can expect that
return.

THE FIRST STEP: AN OUTLINE

Before beginning your business plan, you should write a
detailed outline listing all the topics you will cover.
Use this outline to determine what information you will
need in order to write the business plan, and gather
this information before you begin writing. This

information should include:

- Resumes of your founders and key managers

- Market statistics

- Names of your competitors and information about them

- Material and labor cost data

- Magazine and newspaper articles about your business or industry

- Names of potential customers

- R&D information

- Regulations and laws which could affect your business
- Patent, copyright, and trademark information

You should be careful to organize your business plan in clearly defined sections. Typically, business plans will have separate sections discussing the management team, the product, marketing and sales plans and financial information. These areas are described in more detail in section 3-6 of this guidebook.

Use an outline and stick to it. Be careful not to mix up your subjects. Don't describe the market for a product as you are writing the product description.

THE EXECUTIVE SUMMARY

Venture capitalist investors typically receive numerous business plans each week. Because they may not be willing to research through an entire business plan to locate its essential elements, you should put those essentials in a short introduction called the "executive summary".

Your objective in the executive summary is to convince investors to study your business plan further. The summary should describe all of the key elements for your business plan in just one or two pages. It should include the following critical information:

- A brief description of your product and its estimated market. (Be sure to describe the success ingredient that will make your company unique.)

- A brief description of your management team and how that team will help the company achieve success. Be sure to include successful business ventures you and your team may have been involved in.

- A capsule summary of key projected financial data, such as annual revenue and net income for five years.

- An estimate of the amount of venture capital money
  you are seeking and how you will use the money.

A well-written executive summary allows prospective
investors to decide within two or three minutes if your
plan deserves further study.

Your executive summary has another important use. If
your business plan is lengthy and heavy, it can be
cumbersome to send the entire plan. Instead, if you are
sending your plan to venture capitalists who don't know
you or who might not be interested in what you offer,
you may want to send only the executive summary with a
cover letter. If they read the summary and are
interested in seeing the whole plan, you can then mail
it or present it in person.

This will help protect the confidential details of your
plan and save printing and postage costs.

HOW LONG SHOULD IT BE?

People writing a business plan for the first time
frequently ask, "How long and how detailed should it
be?" There are no fixed rules. Your plan's length will
depend on how much money you are trying to raise and

how sophisticated and complex your company's operations will be. If you are seeking $5 million to start a high-technology manufacturing company you will probably need a highly detailed plan which contains an in-depth market analysis, five-year cost and sales projections, detailed research and development information, and financial data to back up your assumptions and projections.

On the other hand, if you are seeking $100,000 seed capital to research and develop a new product for an existing market, you may be able to tell your story in 15 to 20 pages.

The detail required in your business plan may also depend on who you are and how much experience you have. If you are a seasoned manager with a good track record, a venture capitalist may not require too much information in the early stages. You will nevertheless need to gather all of the above data in the future or before a major second round of financing.

A well known Silicon Valley venture capitalist once said: "Gene Amdahl (found of Amdahl Computer Corporation) could write a business plan on the back of an envelope and every venture capitalist on the West Coast would want to look at it." This may be an

38

overstatement but there is no question that a successful
entrepreneur can interest most venture capitalists
simply by picking up the phone or by writing a short
letter explaining his new proposal.

Many venture capitalists interviewed in the preparation
of this booklet stated that the trend is toward shorter,
less detailed business plans. One respected venture
capitalist said, "The size of a company's business plan
is often inversely proportional to its ability to raise
money." The business plan should cover all of the
important elements, but it need not be several hundred
pages long. As long as you include enough information
to convince venture capitalists you have done your
homework and understand the matter, they will appreciate
a shorter and less detailed plan.

FINISHING TOUCHES

You will need to give some attention to the physical
presentation of your business plan. Remember, your plan
should make it easy for venture capitalists to locate
the information in which they are most likely to be
interested. Your business plan should have a table of
contents to allow the reader to locate any section
quickly and conveniently. You might also consider

placing tabs on the first page of each section identifying the contents of that section. This is more than a simple convenience. Many venture capital groups are made up of three or four people, each with different specialties. After reading the executive summary, one person may want to look at your marketing section first, while another may want to examine your financial data section first.

When you have a completed draft of your business plan, you should ask at least two independent parties to review the plan before you send it to venture capitalists. Your reviewers should understand venture capital deals and be able to give you constructive suggestions. Other entrepreneurs, your accountants, or your attorneys would probably be good reviewers.

Once your business plan is complete, you should give some thought to printing and binding it. Offset printing and expensive binding is not necessary. If your plan is short (less that 25 pages), a simple clear plastic cover with post or slip binders--which can be purchased at any stationery store--is adequate. If your plan is longer, you may want to use a three-ring notebook.

You should remember that an elaborate presentation is not necessary and may not be advisable. Expensive, lavishly prepared plans may make venture capitalists question your priorities. They may also wonder how many copies were made and how many investors besides themselves have seen the plan. Venture capitalists who suspect that your plan has been widely distributed may be less interested, so be careful to make only enough copies for each member of your founding team and for a reasonable number of prospective venture capitalists.(2)

The Market Environment

Dollars attract talent! This is the rule underlying how the electronic data processing industry grew and developed. Nowhere is that more apparent than in the product environment confronting users. A multitude of "mysterious" technological products, promoted by confusing claims of superiority generated by professional marketing machines, confronts anyone intending to acquire high technology products or services.

"The 3 R's" is the bible for sales personnel in any industry:

-- Rapport: having a sympathetic understanding of the user's problems.

-- Rationale: solving those problems with the vendor's product.

-- Relationship: building a market for more product sales.

The electronic data processing industry has brought the 3 R's to a high art. Most sales personnel deal with either technicians who have little or no concept of business, or business people who have a paralyzing fear of technology. The result in both cases is that the sales representative has total control over the transaction. With business people, who approach technology as if dealing with a dread disease, the vendor's marketing representative leverages off computer mystique. Creating the expectation that the product will magically solve the user's problem, pressure is applied to compel a quick but favorable decision. By focusing on the perception that the product's supply is limited because of its popularity, pressure is created through such ploys as:

* Delivery window: sign the contract now and delivery can be promised within a certain period of time; otherwise, there's no telling when this product will be available. (This is effective for those who perceive an immediate need for that product.)

* Price freeze or discount: Immediate execution of the contract will cause the price to be frozen, or will result in a discount. (The chance to save dollars is always an inducement for those prone to quick, short-sighted

decisions.)

These ploys emphasize speed over planning. Little thought is given to assurances of performance. Indeed, there is often blind reliance on the sales representative's bland assurances capped by the phrase "no problem." Instead of carefully understanding the resources at risk, business people are often so glad to either save money or lock-up a delivery date that they take a laisse faire attitude concerning functionality and support.

In dealing with technicians, a free trial to "analyze" the product generally establishes the dependence of a "sudden need." The technician runs to the user's decision-maker bleating that the world will come to an end if the vendor's contract isn't signed immediately, to lock-up use of the product. An even more effective ploy used in dealing with technicians and novice users is the opportunity to become a "beta" (pilot) site. Like a bad sci-five movie, the user finds itself starring in the final phase of a "state-of-the-art" product development. Instead of buying a product of proven functionality, the user gets the opportunity to spend dollars and risk its business environment on a product that may not work. Basically, for a lower than normal cost the product is installed and operated in the user's business.

The vendor has the right to monitor how a product functions and to make changes accordingly. It also has the right to tour

43

potential customers through the user's business environment to show how the product functions. In essence, the user not only pays for the product's final development work but provides the vendor with free advertising. For some reason, the allure of the beta site ploy is irresistible.

For the price of a discount, business people expose their operations to chaos by allowing an unperfected product to process their proprietary data. Perhaps it is the attraction of being on the "leading edge" which impels normally sane business people to rely on a product with uncertain prospects. In any event, all vendor ploys hinge on a basic assumption: trust; the warm and friendly feeling of being able to rely on the solid good faith of the sales representative; knowing that this individual will "be there" when needed. As one executive told me, contracts are just legal gobblygook designed to make lawyers rich--no one pays attention to what they say. Unfortunately, that attitude is common among business people who like to make decisions with minimal interference.

Trust is an important part of the business ethic. The premise is that once the "business issues" are resolved, legal issues will fall into place. After all, if the vendor and end user both want a successful business relationship, then wouldn't the vendor have significant motivation to perform? The answer is a resounding no!

44

The vendor is a business organization who's chief objectives are expeditious payment and insulation from liability. Regardless of how warm and friendly the sales rep, the vendor's objectives control its business relationship. The user has totally different requirements: it wants product performance, support (training and maintenance), and recourse in the event of failure. The difference is a chasm wide enough to swallow Antarctica and just as cold.

Parts apart: The classic example of what can happen to a novice computer buyer is the saga of an auto parts dealer. He was a friendly, successful individual who operated a retail auto parts business with annual sales of over one-half-million dollars. Auto parts is all inventory, requiring constant tracking and re-ordering so that market demand can be satisfied. This person visited a trade show for the auto parts industry, where he noticed a computer system on exhibit, designed just for inventory control and tracking. He asked for a demonstration, was impressed, and executed "all the legal mumbo jumbo" (which included an installment lease contract obligating himself for about $60,000. Subsequently, the system was delivered and installed by the vendor, who left after declaring that it was operational. Three days were spent by his employee trying to understand the manual; thereafter, she started to input data. Two days later, when virtually all inventory information had been pumped into the system, it crashed, wiping out the files.

This happened twice, until the vendor representative casually mentioned "back-up" (over the phone). Even after the data was finally entered, the system would "lock-out" the operator (preventing further processing), or generate "ghost" data (jumbling the files so that no one could determine what inventory actually existed), or crash (wiping out existing files). Frequent complaints to the vendor were met with silence. Finally, aware that inventory was in chaos, unable to meet customer requirements, and with his staff strained to the breaking point, he closed down for a day, hired four temporary people and manually inventoried his stock. He also stopped using the computer, packing and storing it in his warehouse. What really galled him was the fact that beside having reduced his business to chaos, costing him a significant percentage of his market, the obligation to make monthly payments continued, even though the system failed to perform. The installment lease contract contained a "hell or high water" clause in which the bank's right to demand and receive monthly payments was exclusive from the vendor's obligations to perform. This meant that payment obligations were unaffected, even though the product failed to perform and the vendor refused to support user needs. So angered was he by the frustration caused by the unresponsive vendor--who smugly told the user to "stuff it"--he brought the computer to a railroad crossing, laid it across the tracks, and took a picture of the locomotive rushing to crush that "infernal machine."

46

Although he suffered frustration, at least his business survived.   Many other users, confronted with similar circumstances and unable to climb out of the hole, saw their businesses collapse.

Coping: Whether the business be a behometh or tadpole, system performance can affect survival.   A multimillion dollar conglomerate was brought to its knees by a $75,000 software product which "ate" its general ledger data.   It cost that organization over $6 million dollars to reconstruct its files. Employee overtime and consequent trauma were not counted in that dollar figure.   To survive similar disasters requires common sense, and the ability to cope with the market environment to avoid being boxed in by circumstances bereft of support.   This means being able to control decision-making as to produce and vendor selection so that the vendor can be compelled to meet the user's business expectations concerning performance, support, and recourse.

In essence, it is much easier to pay the money than to get it back.   So before relying on the "warm and friendly" sales rep, check out both the vendor and the product.   Make certain that the vendor is reputable and the product has a track record.   The next Chapter will describe the "Acquisition Process," designed to help the decision-maker identify the appropriate product and select a responsive vendor, while formulating a contract that reflects user expectations. Remember, the determinant for investing time and effort in pursuing the acquisition process is not the computer product's dollar cost, but whether it will significantly benefit business operations. Whether the cost is $3,000 or $30,000, the effort is worth the investment in time and resources. As the auto parts dealer discovered, once down, it's tough (and very expensive) to climb out of that chasm.

FOOTNOTES

1   Financing High Technology Growth Situations, Michael A.
    Daniels, Esq., January 20, 1984.

2   Section 2:   The Business Plan Format, "Raising Venture
    Capital: An Entrepreneur's Guidebook" Deloitte Haskins
    & Sells.

NOTES

CHAPTER II

ACQUIRING THE RIGHT TECHNOLOGY

A.   INTRODUCTION

Selecting the "right" technology can be a nerve-wracking experience. The flood of incomprehensible information, competing claims, and bombast makes it virtually impossible to formulate an intelligent business decision. Sorting through this deluge of information has itself produced an industry of consultants who, for hefty fees, will help buyers match technology to their needs. This Chapter is designed to provide guidelines that will help determine which questions should be asked, to whom they should be addressed, what type of answers ought to be expected and how to use those answers in formulating the "right" business decision. In addition, the reader will be provided a guided tour of the why, what, how, when and where of technology acquisition agreements, with special attention paid to the pitfalls awaiting the unwary.

B.   IDENTIFICATION AND SELECTION: PROBLEMS AND SOLUTIONS

Most decisions to acquire technology appear to be made out of frustration and fear instead of through a sensible, well-managed process. The result is often additional and unexpected costs to conform the technology to business needs or, worse, the devastating impact on a business caused by the failure of technology to perform. Avoiding those results means recognizing and coping with problems common to all buyers of high technology products such as the:

(1) <u>Failure of a buyer to formulate its own needs prior to contacting vendors.</u> As previously discussed, the essence of controlling a transaction is knowing business needs. An awareness of the functions that must be performed, as well as of the performance environment, is critical to formulating the needs that technology must satisfy. Prior knowledge of business needs is akin to holding the high ground when confronting technology vendors. To gain that advantage, the buyer must invest the time and resources needed to gather the necessary information about itself. This identification and selection process requires:

(a) A management team able to gather information as to business requirements through a well-organized process that focuses on objectivity. The result should be a listing of functions that must be performed, the resources required to support such performance, the current cost of those resources, and the projected cost over the next three- to five-year period. This listing of functional requirements is called a frame of reference, and it establishes the price/performance ratio that must be satisfied by the vendor's proposed technical solution; and

(b) Communication of that frame of reference to vendors in a manner that concisely conveys the information while maximizing the buyer's competitive leverage with potential vendors.

This is easier said than done! Management is often under pressure to meet short-term goals. Timetables and superiors have to be satisfied. The time value of thinking out a process has to be balanced against the cost of short-run market objectives. Result: the proverbial crucible! Decisions must be made. Time costs money, and the process of selecting the right technology is not as important as meeting market needs. So managers often dispense with the additional stress of dealing with lawyers, accountants, and other "non-business types." Basically, they rely on their ever-constant sales representative to get the product in, put it on line, and start operations--without hassle or delay. Illustrative of this pressure and its potential problems was the line manager for a major insurance company who desired to purchase a license for a low cost software product. He knew the vendor's sales representative, had dealt with him for years, and was satisfied that the product would perform. He could not understand why the insurance company's attorney wanted to change the vendor's standard license agreement. More importantly, he was under pressure to get a job done and could not be bothered with all the legal "nonsense" raised by that attorney. In a meeting, the company's attorney asked that manager the following questions. Did he want:

(a) The software product to perform continuously as represented by the sales material;

(b) The vendor to provide the (training) support promised by the friendly sales representative;

(c) The vendor to expeditiously respond and cure a failure of performance;

(d) To make certain that the product actually worked before he made payment.

In response to those questions the manager answered "yes." The attorney then continued his questioning. Did the manager want:

(e) To pay for loss of the product before it was delivered;

(f) The insurance company exposed to millions of dollars in consequential damages regardless of fault;

(g) To pay for costs, in addition to price, not shown on the invoice; and

(h) The vendor to escape any and all responsibility for a failure to properly cure product performance defects.

To all those questions, the manager answered "no." He and the attorney then reviewed the vendor's standard license agreement and found:

* Hidden costs associated with updates and enhancements;

* Risk of loss, and title passing to the insurance company as soon as the product was loaded on a carrier so the insurance company would be liable for payment regardless of whether the product was damaged on arrival;

* Guarantee of product integrity regardless of fault, so in the event of inadvertent (innocent) disclosure, the insurance company would be liable for

consequential damages;

* No assurance of product performance;

* No assurance of adequate training;

* No assurance of adequate documentation, so that the insurance company personnel may not even be aware of all product functions;

* No assurance that the vendor would cure a failure to product performance within a reasonable period of time, so that the insurance company could "rely" on product performance; and

* Unconditional obligation to make payments to an assignee (third party who purchased the right to receive payments from the insurance company), even if the vendor failed to perform any of its contractual obligations.

It became obvious to the manager that even though the product's cost was small, exposure of the insurance company to liability was overwhelming. The lesson: Expectation must be well formulated and understood in order to reduce risk of performance failure to unanticipated liability. If the manager had signed the contract, he would have had no assurance that the products would have performed in accordance with his expectations. Indeed, the products could have failed totally, and his employer not only would still have been required to pay full price, but would also have been exposed to unlimited liability, regardless of fault. Not the type of dial that makes for long business careers. By using a well-organized process to identify needs and select a responsive vendor, the user avoids hidden costs, liabilities and lack of performance.

Initiating a process designed to gather the appropriate information is the very reason that most business organizations are willing to pay those hefty consultant fees. In the long run, it is cheaper than doing the job with untrained management personnel. Whether the buyer uses a consultant or invests the time and resources to understand its own application requirements, there should be a detailed listing of the elements that constitute each of the applications to be automated. In addition, that listing should include the resources (employees, space, supplies) needed to perform those applications, as well as the time required for completion of each application. The buyer should then project the usage load (information currently processed) and the costs of supporting that usage load over a two- to five-year period. The result is a price/performance ratio giving the buyer a comprehensive idea of the applications being performed, the current information load supported by those applications, the resources needed to maintain that current load, and the projected resources needed to support future load. Those conclusions create a frame of reference, helping the buyer to understand what has to be automated, and when, and the cost benefit expected. With that frame of reference, a buyer should be able to select a vendor, not on the basis of vague promises, but within the reality of specific application needs. Going into the market without that knowledge is like betting your career on a crapshoot.

2.   **Failure of buyers to communicate needs.** It is not enough to know the business applications that must be performed. The buyer must then communicate those needs to vendors. Like the loss of idioms in the translation of languages, communication between vendor and buyer often becomes confused where the latter fails to follow a sensible process. Consider the industrial scale service organization that wanted to computerize its record management system. The company's chief concern was that it be able to certify industrial scales automatically for each of its pharmaceutical customers thirty days before the end of a federally stipulated period. If certification did not so occur, the client could not prove to the federal authorities that the scales were accurate, and this terminated the

client's use of those devices. Naturally, since everything a pharmaceutical company produces has to be weighed at some point in time, an inability to use those scales would put it out of business.

Not having much of a sense of humor, the damaged pharmaceutical company would pursue the industrial scale company for redress of damages. With that picture, we go back to the president of the industrial scale company, who, having read at least one magazine mentioning the word computer, and talked to his brother-in-law (the all knowing accountant), walked into his friendly local neighborhood computer store knowing "exactly" what he wanted. After describing his needs in a "general manner" (he didn't want to give away any unnecessary information), the sales representative suggested a microcomputer and packaged software to handle general ledger and data base management operations.

Known for incisive decision-making, the president of the industrial scale company bought the recommended system, because he felt it would meet his needs and, more importantly, it was cheap! He paid $12,000 for the system, had it installed, pumped in data, and found that his secretary could type faster than the system could process information. It was so slow that ten seconds elapsed before a command was processed. Result: it took an hour to track a simple change in schedule. The president was furious. How could the retailer sell him a product that processed information so slowly? More time would be spent waiting for the system to process scale service changes than the actual time spent in servicing those changes. The retailer pleaded "its not my job to customize systems, I sell'em as they are." Poor communication! Like ships passing in the night, neither side connected. Instead, they talked past each other, focusing on their own perspectives without passage of an "understanding."

The retailer didn't know or care about the buyer's business needs, and the latter was so wrapped up in his own ego that he could not see past a clerk's incantation of technical phrases to find lack of comprehension. This is typical of buyers who believe they don't need expertise to understand and communicate their technical requirements.

In another incident, the vendor's proposal was highly technical. To read it required at least two degrees in engineering and maybe language qualification in Sanskrit. Clearly, the vendor was brilliant, and just as clearly, he couldn't communicate his way out of a paper bag. This meant that besides not being understood, he probably couldn't understand the user's business requirements, as, in fact, proved to be the case. The latter, taken by all the technical mumbo jumbo, agreed to the vendor's proposal and found that cost overruns and mismanagement were common problems to those interested only in solving technical problems. In fact, this user almost went bankrupt before finally calling a halt and bringing in a more business-oriented vendor. Lesson: communication is a two-way street. Both sides have to fully understand the other's requirements. No matter how brilliant the vendor, if it can't communicate in an intelligent, clear and comprehensive (business-like) manner, then it is not going to understand the buyer's needs. The result, of course, would be an unmitigated disaster for the buyer who would not only fail to get the appropriate technology, but as with the above example, end-up spending more than anticipated.

REQUEST FOR PROPOSAL

To avoid any such failure to communicate, professionals--representing buyers--use a device known as a Request For Proposal (RFP). Designed to provide appropriate information in a clear and concise manner, the RFP is the standard document used to convey and request information. It is divided into two sections: one providing information about the buyer, which the vendor needs in order to provide an appropriate technical solution; and the other supplying information about the vendor, which the buyer needs to evaluate the credibility of the proposed technical solution.

1.   Information About the Buyer:

(a) Identity, size, history, products and growth expectations;

(b) Application objectives, describing the methods used and resources needed to perform the applications that the buyer desires to automate. (Be specific about current cost of performance. Include all elements, such as usage load, current application completion time, support resources (such as employees, space and supply requirements);

(c) Time expectation for automating the applications in point (don't create a time crunch). Remember to provide a layer of additional time in case one of those ever-present "glitches" creates an unexpected delay;

(d) Current cost requirements to perform applications;

(e) Projected growth of application demands over the next two- to five-year period;

(f) Name of a liaison who the vendor may contact in the

event it has questions.

The above information should be as detailed as possible. Technical application requirements for the business functions in point, provided by consultants, can often add to the effectivenss of an RFP.

2.   Information From the Vendor

The major portion of an RFP consists of requests for information that must be provided by the vendor.

(a) Identify, full corporate name, and (if either a subsidiary or affiliate) the parent company's full name. (This is important because a conglomerate can often "milk" subsidiaries, depleting resources and crippling their ability to perform. The result is that the buyer is misled into believing it is dealing with a substantial conglomerate when, in reality, its expectations are supported by a corporate shell.) If the vendor is a subsidiary or affiliate, the buyer should request a capitalization assurance letter from the parent. This document indicates that as of a certain, recent date specified in the RFP, the subsidiary has X ($) amount of capitalizations. This provides a degree of assurance to the buyer that the vendor has the resources to perform.

(b)   Identity of the principals, with biographies and a brief description of the vendor's history and earnings growth over the past two years.   This information should describe the organization's depth, in key personnel as well as financially.   For instance, if the software vendor is a two-man organization and the responsibilities involved might require the constant attention of key personnel (customizing and documenting code), a legitimate question would be whether the vendor has the resources to handle the buyer's transaction in addition to its other client obligations.

(c)   Description of the vendor's technical solution to the buyer's business application requirements.   This description should detail the information processing methodology used by the software vendor, to include data files; the sequence of processing; the layout for each file, screen and report; as well as disk file organization.   In addition, if computer equipment is involved, the vendor should provide a full description of the equipment and its specifications, as well as assurance of compatibility with the software.   (In a multi-vendor transaction the buyer should insist that one vendor be solely responsible for the entire system.   The intent is to assure acquisition of an integrated system consisting of hardware and software, not just the separate hardware and software components.)

(d) Track record of the product in the buyer's particular business environment. The buyer should avoid having to change its pattern of doing business in order to accommodate an inflexible system package. A track record in the buyer's environment indicates an ability to accommodate that particular set of business expectations.

(e) Training support requirements such as the duration, type of personnel to be educated, methodology, cost and location. In addition, the vendor should indicate the functions that will be described to the personnel being trained. (The buyer should also request assurance that the employees who are trained can in fact operate the system.)

(f) Description of maintenance, identifying the limits of maintenance service, response time for service requests, cure-time period and contingencies available to process data in the event cure fails (within that time period). In addition, the vendor should describe cost, duration of the initial maintenance term, party responsible for maintenance of the overall system and ratio of field installations to maintenance service facilities in the buyer's geographic area. (The latter should give the buyer a rough idea of whether the vendor has the resources to meet emergency maintenance requirements. For instance, if the vendor has 500 installations in the buyer's geographic area and only four maintenance service peronnel, it doesn't take a genius to conclude that emergency maintenance resources are non-existent.)

(g)   Assurance that use of the system will not expose the buyer and its employees to toxic hazards. The last thing a buyer needs is a dangerous product; yet some technology may expose users to physical danger (electric shock, chemical mutant agents, etc.) For that reason, the vendor should indicate that the technology does not pose a physical hazard and that no record of any such concern exists with the U.S. Environmental Protection Agency. (Union pressure to restrict employee use of CRT's has gained momentum recently, because of reports that dangerous levels of x-rays are emitted from some devices. Assurance of non-hazardous effect can be used to avert potential labor strife.)

(h)   Field installation references in the buyer's immediate geographic area. The vendor should identify users of the proposed technological solution located in close proximity to the buyer. (These references should be thoroughly checked to avoid "misunderstanding" about the performance claims for that solution. Personal visits are the only way to use effectively the information provided by such references.)

(i) Credit references to indicate that the vendor has the financial resources to support its contractual obligations. (These should be thoroughly checked, by personal visits to the credit source.)

The vendor should be required to use non-technical language in describing its solution, answer all questions in a clear and concise manner, and provide its proposal within a specific time frame. (Failure to meet those requirements demonstrates a sloppy organization that may not be able to understand the buyer's needs, let alone effectively support the technological solution.)

The vendor should be instructed to respond to the RFP within a particular time frame. Two types of responses should be sought: (1) a letter indicating that a proposal will be forthcoming within a particular period of time; and (2) the proposal that is to be provided within the given period of time following that initial "interest" letter.

The RFP should state that: (1) all information received is the property of the buyer (subject to its discretion); (2) the information contained in the proposal will not be considered confidential unless specifically identified as such by the vendor; and (3) the RFP is not a contract and does not in any way bind the buyer to any obligations, or impose liability for any costs, or expenses incurred by the vendor in creating the proposal.

Attached to the RFP, there should be a contract or, at the least, a description of the legal requirements necessary to meet the buyer's business expectations, such as acceptance testing, payment geared to performance, single vendor responsibility (in multi-vendor situations), and contingencies to avert damage in the event of performance failure.

A cover letter should accompany the RFP. It should repeat the instructions regarding clear, concise and non-technical language. It should also affirm the time periods and identify a liaison whom the vendor can contact if it has any questions.

D. THE RFP PROCESS

(1) Leverage: Formulating the RFP and delivering it to vendors is only the first step in a process designed to provide technology that conforms to the buyer's business expectations. Remember, the RFP has two major goals: one is to communicate needs effectively, the other is to build a competitive environment that will motivate vendors to change their business position--in essence, leverage! It does no one any good to describe business expectations if there is no assurance that they will be met. Hence, the need to assure a "responsive attitude" by vendors who believe that the opportunity presented by the

buyer is worth the risk of "changing position."

   (2) <u>Vendor/Buyer Conflict</u>:   When the phrase "changing position" is used, it means that someone is willing to trade greater legal exposure for an opportunity. With a vendor, such a change means a deviation from the business objectives of no liability for performance, and payment up front. For a user, it means payment only for performance, and full recourse (against the vendor) in the event of failure. Clearly, diametrically opposed positions. Getting a change requires motivation (leverage.) For the vendor, such leverage could be:

   (1) Acknowledgement by the buyer that the technology offered is unique; that there is no competition--in other words: the only game in town. Technicians often suggest this conclusion after finding the "right" vendor. Take the DP manager for an insurance company who saw the "dream" software product at a trade show. He immediately told his superior that this hot new product was better than anything else on the market. With that as the sole basis for their "in-depth" finding, they advised the company's attorney that there was no other option but to sign the contract "as is." Such action is typical of technicians who make business decisions. They look only at the immediate technical problem, and ignore the business context in which their technical solution must function. The insurance company accordingly

signed a tight license agreement, paying top dollar for a product that was subsequently discounted to other buyers who (remarkably) found competition.

(2) Acknowledgement by the buyer that the vendor has such superior maintenance that failure to cure within a reasonable period of time will be guaranteed. (This is a play-it-safe conclusion drawn by those who are willing to pay a high price for "proven" technology and a support organization with a reputation that fosters confidence. IBM is often chosen over other vendors for this particular reason, and unless circumstances are unique, it is very difficult to amend the IBM contract.)

(3) Acknowledgement by the buyer that severe time restraints impair its ability to find alternative vendors. (This is an example of short-term objectives overriding long-range objectives--or management-by-crisis. For example, a system's manager at a bank was under considerable pressure to get a project "on-line." He contacted only one vendor, who said it could do the job if the money was paid "up-front." When the bank's attorney complained that there were no assurances of performance, the manager said he "had no time to negotiate, since he needed the system now!" Money was therefore paid to a vendor who could not do the job, necessitating the payment of even more money to a substitute

vendor.)

(4) Acknowledgement by the buyer that it has invested so much time and resources with one vendor that it is unable to consider other alternatives. (This is a ploy successfully used by sales representatives to lead users down the "garden path." In essence, the users are promised everything they want by the sales representative. With those promises the users are drawn into an ever-lengthening discussion of the project's details. As time passes and resources are invested in what appears to be a certainty of expectations, contract discussions are delayed as a detail to be worked out by attorneys. Finally, after several months of detailed discussions the buyer's attorney is told that the vendor's contract cannot be changed to reflect the matters discussed. In fact, the attorney is advised that it is "take it or leave it." Those discussions with the sales representative? Best efforts: he will "try" to get the user what it wants, but no promises. The result is that the buyer has invested so much time and resources that starting all over again would be prohibitive. This is a common trap, particularly for buyers who use inexperienced consultants, since the latter are mislead into believing that their client can get everything it wants without the need for legal assistance.)

Coping with vendor leverage requires advance planning

71

and a commitment to an effort that will require time and persistence. As previously indicated, the first step is to know business application needs. Then create an RFP that effectively communicates those needs, while building a competitive environment. (This means vendors competing for the buyer's business.) With that "competitive element" the buyer has created a feeling of anxiety, worry that someone else will be more responsive. A competitive environment maximizes the buyer's existing leverage, which might be:

(a) <u>Amount of money involved</u>. A direct relationship exists between large dollar amounts and vendor motivation.

(b) <u>Method of payout</u>. Vendors lose money on installment payments, because they generally sell the "receivables" to gain immediate cash flow. For that reason, payout in lump-sum dollar amounts stimulates vendors to be responsive.

(c) <u>Subsequent business</u>. If the follow-up business looks long-term, the vendor can bank on consistent cash flow. The result is a preference for buyers that generate extended follow-up business.

(d) <u>Marketing tools</u>. Buyers with market credibility can help the vendor sell its products. Well-known organizations, industries in particular, are considered influence centers. If they buy the vendor's product, others in that same industry might follow suit. For that reason, acquiring an influential buyer is worth greater vendor flexibility. Another marketing tool that motivates the vendor is acquiring a buyer in a new market. Using that buyer's name, the vendor will be able to penetrate that market more effectively, because the vendor has a "track record."

Vendors are also motivated by being able to "demonstrate" new products to potential markets. For example, if a product is state of the art and has no record of on-site use, then the vendor is unable to show product credibility. If, however, a buyer is willing to permit use of that product at its site in return for being a "demonstration site" for the product (to the vendor's potential customers), then there is significant motivation for a vendor to change its position.

MAINTENANCE COMPETITIVE PRESSURE

Once leverage is identified, the buyer should initiate a plan to maintain the competitive environment and gradually increase pressure on vendors. As a telescope focuses vision, so the process should focus competitive pressure, increasing intensity at various stages until the remaining vendors are fully responsive.

To increase pressure, the buyer uses the selection process as follows:

(1) Send the RFP to the largest number of vendors. A rule-of-thumb is that one in four recipients will respond. The objective is to gain an appropriate response from at least seven vendors.

(2) After receipt of proposals, call a bidders' conference. Invite all participating vendors. The announced purpose is to brief all vendors on the criteria for considering proposals. Actually, the purpose is to create anxiety by compelling each vendor to acknowledge its competition. The buyer puts on a "dog-and-pony show," reiterating some of the major facts in the RFP (who it is, its application problems, etc.) Only mundane (and irrelevant) questions will be asked, the vendor sales representatives being too busy noting their opposite numbers. After the buyer's presentation, vendor sales representatives will attempt personal contact—with invitations to lunch, demonstrations (and lunch) or invitations to dinner. All such invitations should be cordially rejected as being

inappropriate. The buyer's aloofness will increase its competitive environment.

(3) After the bidders' conference comes the individual demonstrations. The obstensible purpose is for each vendor to describe fully (and, if possible, demonstrate) its technical solutions. During the vendor's presentation (usually by the sales representative) the buyer should ask questions based on proposals received from other vendors. The objective is to cut through the hype and pin the vendor down on comparative specifics. In addition, the buyer should request the name of the vendor's decision-maker, defined as the individual who can bind the vendor to changes in its contract. Generally, the sales representative will be evasive, arguing that it is in the buyer's interest to deal through the representative (since, after all, it is the representative who best understands the buyer's needs). The buyer should use this opportunity to draw lines of authority, insisting on the decision-maker's name, and indicating that the representative will be a conduit to the vendor but not its negotiator.

During this second stage, the questions should produce a degree of tension. To avoid damaging the manager's relationship with the vendor, all questions should be generated by the buyer's attorney. With only a temporary involvement in the process, the attorney can be a lightening rod, drawing enmity, while fully insulating the manager from any ill-feelings generated by intensifying the competitive environment.

(4) After completing the presentations, vendor prospects should be haled. A second bidders' conference should be convened, obstensibly to discuss the buyer's basic concerns with any future relationship, basically performance, responsiveness and recourse. Again, the purpose is to intensify existing competitive pressure by demonstrating that the buyer will: (a) analyze competitive proposals, except any that are considered inappropriate; and (b) put a premium on performance and recourse. The vendor's reaction during the first should be mirrored in the second (general questions and attempts at personal contact with the manager).

(5) The buyer's attorney should then contact each of the remaining vendors and indicate that, in addition to technical solutions, the vendors must be responsive to the buyer's legal requirements reflected in the RFP. The attorney's letter should require a written response, within a described period of time, to each of the legal considerations contained in the RFP. (It is assumed that virtually all proposals would avoid a direct response to the buyer's legal contract or described considerations).

(6) The final selection of vendors is made on the basis of vendors' response to the attorney's letter, in addition to its technical solutions and business credibility. The final selection consists of two vendors. Buyers often designate them as primary and alternate. Such designation is not only offensive (particularly to the alternate vendor) but actually detracts from the attempt to intensify competitive pressures, since the designated "alternate" no longer has the same motivation to respond. Experience shows that it is unnecessary to make any designation. Simply indicate to both that they are close and that a decision will be made on the basis of which vendor: (a) has the best technical solution,   (b) demonstrates the highest degree of business credibitility; and (c) is most responsive to the buyer's legal requirements (underlying implementation of its business needs).

(7) Negotiations should continue with both vendors, simultaneously, advising each that the other is just as responsive (or more so) to the buyer's business requirements. Again, the attorney is taking the lead in communicating with each vendor, thereby insulating the manager's future business relationship from any potential enmity. This stage requires that the greatest amount of finesse, since a vendor could become so frustrated as to quit, leaving the carefully orchestrated competitive climate in shambles. So it is

critically important to treat each vendor as if it is the leading prospect. (Even if this is not so, use the "strawman" ploy to create that perception.) At the conclusion of this step, the buyer should have concluded a contract with a vendor that not only provides the best technical solution, but is also fully responsive to the vendor's legal requirements.

A rule-of-the-thumb is that (between two vendors), where one has the best technical solution but is not fully responsive to legal requirements, and the other has an adequate technical solution and is more responsive, the second vendor is preferred. The reason is obvious: the best system in the world is worthless if the buyer cannot get the vendor to maintain performance.

F. CONSIDERING COST BENEFIT

The process of identifying and maximizing leverage requires a commitment of time and money. Small or middle-sized businesses of ten argue that they cannot afford the cost of hiring lawyers or consultants to implement or pursue that process. The process is perceived as being more expensive than the system being acquired. That may be true. Creating a competitive environment and intensifying pressures is expensive. The question is: when is it worth committing the resources to pursue that process? Obviously, if one is acquiring a single off-the-shelf software package for use on a microcomputer, it makes no sense to implement that process. But, if the technology is essential to business operations, then failure to perform could be severely damaging. In that circumstance, it makes no difference whether the technology costs $10,000 or $100,000, since business integrity is at stake whatever the cost. Where that situation exists, the expense of pursuing this process is worth every dime, since the assurance of technological performance protects the overall value of the business, which is the ultimate benefit derived from such technology.

G. A TURNKEY SYSTEM CONTRACT CHECKLIST

Following is an extract from the book **OEM AND TURNKEY CONTRACTS**, published by Carnegie Press, and written by Leonard F. Turi, who is a nationally-known business systems consultant with over twenty years of experience in helping organizations select technology that meets their needs. This checklist is designed to help the reader understand the complexity involved in the process of analyzing business needs.

CHECKLIST: CONSIDERATIONS IN A TURNKEY SYSTEMS CONTRACT*

1. Equipment

    - Identified by Component

    - Price and Term

    - Replacement Parts

    - Payment

    - Option to Purchase

    - Delivery

    - Installation

    - Expansion Capabilities

    - Price Protection - Current Prices

    - Price Protection - Future Hardware

    - Partial Deliveries

    - Warranty of New Equipment

    - Pass Through of Investment Tax Credit

    - Trade-in Credits

    - Communication Capabilities

2. Operating System Software

    - Version

    - Language(s) Supported

    - License to Use

3.   Report Software (Application Programs)

- List of Sample Reports

- List of Programs

   a. Report Generators

   b. Edit Runs

   c. Miscellaneous

   d. Frequency

- Modification to Programs

- Price Protection - Software Enhancements

- Maintenance Responsibility

- License to Use

- Development of Software

   a. Ownership

   b. Royalties

- User Right to Source Code

- Title and Ownership

- Programming Review

- Right to Use Software in Other Locations

4.   Installation

- Installation Schedule - Critical Path Method

- Responsibilities with Scheduled and Actual Dates

   for Commencement and Completion

- Conversion Techniques

   a. Client and Matter Master Files

   b. Client and Matter Numbering

        c. Attorney Master File

        d. Tables

            (1) Area of Law

            (2) Time Codes

- Check Points

- Percentage Completion by Phase and Tasks

- Rights to Cancel at Phase Ends

- Deliverables by Phase

- Installation Costs

- Transportation Costs

- Staffing Requirements

- Documentation

        a. Operator's manual

        b. Run Book

        c. Lawyer Manual

- Progress Reports

- Vendor Time Records

- Supply Specifications

- Supply Sources

- No Subcontracting without Contract

- Amount of Training to be Supplied by Vendor

- Training Materials to be Supplied

- Location of Training

- Reliance on Vendor Expertise

5.   Maintenance (Equipment)

   - Prevention Maintenance

   - Hours of Maintenance

   - Response Time

   - Location of Spare Parts

   - Repair Parts

   - Cost

   - Malfunction Report

6.   Maintenance (Software)

   - Operating System

   - Application Programs

   - Warranties

   - Rights to Enhancements

   - Response Time

7.   Acceptance Tests (Hardware and Software)

   - Are They Complete and Thorough?

   - Acceptance Testing Before Installation of
     Equipment

   - Acceptance Testing After Installation of
     Equipment

   - Acceptance Test Failure Actions

   - Payment Conditions

   - Testing Monthly and Quarterly Reports

8. Site Planning

   - Site Preparation Responsibilities

      a. Electrical

      b. Space

      c. Humidity (Static)

      d. Noise Control

      e. Air Filtration

      f. Storage

      g. Temperature

      i. Air Conditioning (BTU'S)

   - Site Drawings

9. Warranties/Remedies

   - Equipment

   - Software

   - Maintenance

   - Expressed and Implied Warranties

   - UCC Applicability

   - Indemnification

   - Inclusion of Cots in Indemnity

   - Risk of Loss at All Stages

   - Limitation of Liability

   - Quiet Enjoyment

   - Force Majeure (Cancellation Rights)

   - Disaster Recovery

   - Patent and Copyright Indemnity

- Rights in Default

- Assignment by Vendor and/or User

- Notice

- Confidentiality

- Damage to Equipment

- Pass Through of Supplier Warranties

- Notice of Default and Right to Cure

- Liquidation Damages for Delays

- All Amendments in Writing

- Authority

- Entire Agreement

- Governing Law and Forum

- No Liens or Encumbrances

- Arbitration

10. Other Provisions

- Most Favored Customer

- Delivery Deferral Rights

- Delivery Acceleration Rights

- Delay Impact

- Price Reductions or Discounts

- Title Transfer

- User and Vendor Confidentiality

- Bankruptcy of Vendor

- Events of Default

- Termination Rights

- Continuity During Disputes
- Cancellation Costs
- Performance Bond
- Insurance Requirements
- Access by Auditors
- Right to Use System Anywhere
- Right to Use System in Any Way

* Compliments of Frank Aretowicz, Jr. and Ward Bower, Altman & Weil, Inc., from their book **LAW OFFICE AUTOMATION & TECHNOLOGY**, New York: Matthew Bender, 1981

H.   IMPORTANCE OF THE CONTRACT

The process of maximizing the competitive environment is designed to yield a contract responsive to the buyer's business needs.   Management personnel, beset with operations daily pressures, are often willing to listen to the siren song of sales representatives who argue that the best contract is one that is put away and forgotten.   Their point is that the vendor has to do a good job to maintain credibility.   Otherwise it stands a good chance of going out of business.   So, even if these sales representatives maintain, the contract is one-sided and unfair, that is unimportant, because the vendor will meet the buyer's expectations in order to expand its market credibility.   There is some truth in this, but the real question is: if the vendor doesn't think the contract is significant and is not going to follow the buyer's business expectations, why doesn't it sign a contract closer to those expectations? The answer is that old shell game of "now you see it and now you don't." Vendors want to create the illusion of meeting the buyer's needs without actually being bound to do so. A classic example of this illusion at work is the saga of the president for a small manufacturing company who prided himself on negotiating his own deals. Confident of his own abilities, he felt that outsiders, such as lawyers, consultants or accountants, would get in the way. Needing to meet certain volume orders quickly, he called a "couple of vendors" to discuss automating his manufacturing facility. One computer hardware representative convinced him that a multi-vendor set-up (separate hardware and software vendors) would solve his problems. With this as the decisive factor, and only a cursory demonstration of how the actual product was to function, the manufacturer signed multiple agreements with two vendors (prepared by those vendors). The hardware vendor received a contract for equipment and maintenance of that equipment. The software vendor (recommended by the hardware vendor's sales representative) received signed contracts for software and maintenance. The total cost to the manufacturer was to be $75,000. Unfortunately, none of those agreements were integrated, reflecting the other. This produced contracts for separate items, not for an integrated system. As a consequence, as the pieces (hardware and software) were delivered, no one vendor was responsible for putting them together. Complaints from the manufacturer were answered with that sonorous phrase "it isn't in the contract." (Remember how unimportant the contract was to the vendor at the time it was selling to the buyer). As a consequence, with those volume order deadlines approaching, the manufacurer sat there with pieces of a system that neither vendor would assemble without additional compensation. What was worse, after the manufacturer capitulated and paid the extra ($25,000) to have the system assembled, neither vendor would assume responsibility for servicing the integrated system. As a result, each time a problem occurred, the manufacturer was thrown into a frenzy of effort, cajoling the two vendors into keeping the system in operation. Often, the manufacturer could assure results only through additional (non-maintenance) payments. The final bill for that $75,000 system was more than double that amount. This sum did not include the time lost by the manufacturer from operating this business, because of the "friendly, no problem" technical solution recommended by the hardware vendor. In addition (adding insult to injury), in spite of the added maintenance costs, the system never performed fully in accordance with expectations.

This saga of cost overruns, poor performance, and uncooperative vendors, all threatening the operation integrity of a business, is not unusual. The manufacturer failed to: (1) require that the contract reflect his performance expectations;

and (2) require recourse in the event of poor performance. He did not consider his own needs important enough to require a document assuring their satisfaction.

Small businesses, or technically naive people, are not the only ones who fall into the trap of believing that the vendor will meet user expectations regardless of the contract. A conglomerate with annual sales of over 300 million dollars needed a software system to perform all bookkeeping functions. Its vice president of operations contacted a small software house that had developed such a system and was willing to sell "cheap." (Shades of the industrial scale president.) The conglomerate's general counsel advised that VP to sign the vendor's standard contract because "we're big and no one's going to mess with us." The conglomerate signed the vendor's standard contract, paid the $75,000 license fee, installed the software without back-up, and found the product was inadequate. Within the first month the company was unable to process receivables, payables, inventory, or virtually any of the data relating to the conglomerate's internal operations. Since they had no automated back-up, they had to rely on manual operations, which quickly swamped them in a deluge of paper. Administrative operations ground to a halt. Management didn't know who was paying them or for what, which products were in stock, what money was owed and to whom, or the status of all the innumerable considerations that are essential to operating an organization of such magnitude. In effect, they were technically out of business! From the chairman of the board on down, everyone was galvanized into extraordinary efforts to save the business. Over seven million dollars was spent in hiring consultants to restructure both data lost and processing operations. This sum was in addition to the lost business and the weakening of market position caused by poor inventory control and marketing support. Nor did it include the hundreds of thousands of dollars in overtime spent working with those consultants to restore the integrity of the conglomerate. Anger and frustration generated by that circumstance was expressed in a $22 million lawsuit filed by the conglomerate against that small software vendor ($100,000 in assets). What chance did that small, weak vendor have against the virtually unlimited resources of a multi-million dollar conglomerate? In this case "muscle" lost! The conglomerate was compelled to settle for return of its license fee ($75,000). Why, because the contract limited the vendor's liability to that amount, and the buyer was bound by that contract. Lesson: no matter how big or small, the contract binds! So the importance of a contract is (no matter what the vendor says): it is the written word that binds. If that word is to reflect performance expectations, it had better be in the contract.

I. ANATOMY OF A CONTRACT

The function of a contract is to describe the transaction. Drafting that description means outlining what has to occur and when, and assurance of occurrence and recourse for failure. In essence, a contract is the instruction manual for implementing and completing the transaction. This means that any such contract must be detailed to indicate the what, when, where, how and why of the transaction. The key rule in drafting is to "get it all in writing."

A case which reflects the importance of that rule is IBM v. Catamore. In that case, the buyer--Catamore--signed three contracts with IBM: one for hardware, another for software, and a third for support. Catamore's intent was to acquire a turnkey system. Unfortunately, none of the contracts contained any integrating language reflecting a combination of components. Indeed, each had language indicating an exclusivity and independence from any other agreement. After the hardware and software were delivered, Catamore requested IBM to assemble and install the "integrated system." IBM's response was that such obligation was not in the contract. Catamore brought suit, arguing that it would not have acquired the hardware and software components if they were not to be assembled into an integrated and fully compatible unit. The lower court agreed with IBM that such duty of assembly was not in any contract. As expected, the court found those three separate agreements to be independent and exclusive, without any inter-relationship. Although Catamore eventually won on other grounds, the lower court's ruling that an inter-relationship was excluded because it wasn't in writing, was not disturbed. So, make certain that all promises of performance are fully described in the written agreement, or they may just evaporate after the last friendly handshake, just as the check is passed to the vendor.

The basics that should be in any contract are:

(1) Identification of the product and description of the performance specifications. The vendor's use of a name or numerical product identification should be expanded to include the product's functional performance specification. For software, this means documentation describing the application program's narrative, as well as its file, screen and report layout, disk organization and methodology. This establishes a standard of performance that is the basis for determining product performance. In effect, it automatically creates an express warranty. This means that if the software does not perform in accordance with the specifications described in the contract, then it is not the product that the user intended to acquire. This automatically voids the contract and requires the vendor to return all monies. The product performance specifications do not have to be

physically incorporated into the agreement. Instead, they can be annexed to the agreement by reference. In effect, the contract identifies the performance specifications as a certain exhibit (e.g. Exhibit I) and then indicates that such Exhibit I is annexed to and incorporated by reference into the agreement. The buyer merely has to mark the documentation containing the performance specifications as an exhibit, and they are automatically integrated into the agreement.

Another consideration is the structure of the software's performance specifications. The buyer should insist that those specifications be designed in such a manner that any competent programmer could understand the syntax, logic and methodology. Otherwise, even though the performance specifications will be available, they may not be easily understood by anyone except the original vendor. Such a result is called "locked-in." An example of lock-in concerns a brokerage house that hired a small software company to write a new program for on-line access to customer accounts. The program was written, supplied to the buyer (source code and documentation), installed on the mainframe, and began operation. The vendor's two-week vacation started simultaneously with the software installation. Problems began to arise. The vendor did not answer its phone. The buyer decided to have its technical people correct the problems. After hours of trying to understand the software's logic, syntax and methodology the buyer's technical staff reported failure. The vendor's programming methodology was confusing, illogical and virtually impossible to understand. The buyer then called in the best system analysts money could buy. They thoroughly reviewed the documentation and came up with the same conclusion. The buyer was stuck. When the vendor returned from vacation, the buyer demanded that all problems be solved. The vendor agreed, but at substanital time and material rates. Result, the buyer was locked into perpetuating a poorly written software product. Don't let that happen. Have the vendor certify in writing that a reasonably competent programmer can understand the program's methodology.

The RFP and Proposal should also be attached to and made part of the contract. Those documents detail the history of the transaction and describe the buyer's performance expectations. One of the first signs that the vendor will not cooperate is often a failure to permit incorporation of those documents.

Take the case of the vendor who submitted a proposal that was fully responsive to all questions asked, except reference to the contract. When asked why it did not respond to the contractual provisions attached to the RFP, the vendor stipulated that it used only its standard agreement, which excluded the RFP and Proposal. The vendor not only refused to annex the RFP, but excluded its own proposal because it felt that the sales language was too "broad" for incorporation in the contract. It was akin to saying that false representations are fine for purposes of inducement, but don't expect them to be honored after the contract is signed. In that situation, the vendor lost any opportunity to compete for the buyer's business, but how many times have buyers been fooled by slick proposals into signing tight contracts that deliver less than initially promised? So the lesson is make certain that the RFP and Proposal are part of the contract. Any sign of hesitancy should be taken as a warning about vendor credibility.

(2) Requirement that delivery be completed "inside" at the buyer's installation site. In most vendor contracts, the delivery requirement states "F.O.B. point-of-shipment." This means that risk of loss passes when the product is loaded onto a carrier. Risk of loss means an obligation to pay for the product regardless of condition. The F.O.B. point-of-shipment language indicates that this risk passes to the buyer the moment the product is in place on a carrier. So if the product is damaged in transit, it is the buyer's responsibility. Take the case of Ewing vs. Ball which illustrates the period of F.O.B. point-of-shipment. In that

case, Ewing was a New York manufacturer who wanted to acquire a computer. Naturally, he chose a California company and signed the standard vendor contract, which contained the F.O.B. point-of-shipment clause. The computer was shipped, arrived damaged, and Ewing refused to pay. The vendor sued and won, with the court holding that at the point where the computer was loaded on the carrier all risk during transit passed to the buyer.

Avoid Ewing's error. Change the F.O.B. point-of-shipment clause to read F.O.B. point-of-destination, and define that destination as the buyer's installation site. In that way, the vendor retains all risk during transit and the buyer is assured that there will be no liability if the product arrives in a damaged condition.

(3) A statement that acceptance will occur only if the buyer is assured that the product performs in accordance with performance specifications. Where software is concerned, an additional requirement qualifying performance is the inquiry/response time period (the time it takes to receive a response after inputting information). There should be a limit of four to six seconds for any such response. Exceptions should be well documented in the performance specifications. Together, the performance specifications and the response/inquiry time period should create an "Up-Time

standard," which denotes performance in accordance with expectations. Failure to meet that Up-Time standard should be defined as a failure of performance, or a defect. In the event of a defect, the buyer should be able to reject the product and get its money back, if the vendor is unable to cure within a specified period of time.

Software development requires an acceptance process that assures performance in accordance with expectations. Such a process will require:

(a) The drawing of functional performance specifications in accordance with the buyer's expectations as expressed in the RFP (amplifying the importance of attaching that document to the contract). The vendor should have a defined time limit with which it is comfortable. Failure to meet that time limit would be a breach permitting the buyer to terminate the agreement and receive a refund. The buyer should never "accept" the functional specifications, since it does not have the technical expertise to know if that document meets its expectations. Indeed, the vendor should "sign-off" through a written certification indicating that the functional specifications conform to those expectations. Upon receipt of such certification the buyer and seller should fix a price for the value of those functional specifications. In the event of any subsequent breach, the buyer would want to retain those specifications to assist any future vendor.

(b) Coding in accordance with those functional specifications. The vendor would have a certain agreed upon period of time to complete all program coding. Again, a failure would give the buyer a right to terminate for breach, with the return of all monies, except for the cost of the functional performance specifications. Completion of coding occurs after the buyer receives a written certification from the vendor that the coding accurately reflects the functional performance specifications.

(c) Unit testing at the vendor's location is the next step. The vendor tests each software program, using "live" (existing) data provided by the buyer. In addition, such testing would include hypothetical data designed to emulate stress (high data load) situations. The vendor would test the software on the identical equipment operated by the buyer. During this unit testing period, the buyer would have its representatives at the vendor's location observing the testing procedures. Completion is again based on a certification by the vendor that the software programs demonstrated no defects, or that all defects were corrected and the software programs function in accordance with their respective performance specifications.

(d) System testing at the vendor's site follows unit testing. In that procedure, the vendor tests all the software programs operating together in an integrated and fully compatible unit (system). Again, the vendor uses the buyer's same live and hypothetical data for the system testing as was used in the unit testing. This testing procedure is completed only after the vendor provides the same certification as it did for the software program units.

(e) After unit and system testing at the vendor's location has been completed the process is repeated at the buyer's site, with training tied into the testing period. At that point there should be few if any defects. A failure of performance should mean cure within a relatively short period of time. Inability to cure within prescribed time periods would be cause for rejection and termination by the buyer. Again, after the testing period has been completed and the vendor has provided a written certification that the software performs in accordance with its functional specifications, the buyer can accept and make final payment.

Throughout the acceptance period, payment is geared to performance. For example, ten percent should be paid on execution of the agreement, fifteen percent on receipt of the functional specifications, twenty-five percent on completion of system testing at the vendor's site, and the remainder after acceptance. Although those periodic payment percentages can vary, a rule-of-thumb is that the vendor's profit is thirty percent of the contract price. By holding back at least that percentage, the buyer can assure itself that the vendor will be motivated to perform.

J.   OEM AND MULTI-VENDOR AGREEMENTS

An OEM is known as an Other Equipment Manufacturer--one who adds software to the hardare and sells the whole package as a "turnkey" system. Multi-vendor agreements consist of multiple contracts with separate vendors, each providing a piece (hardware or software) of the total system. Obviously, single-vendor responsibility provided by the OEM avoids the problem of "who's in charge," in implementing the process of acquiring multiple component systems. In a multiple vendor situation it is more difficult for the user to impose accountability for a failure involving more than one component, since each vendor can claim it is the other's problem.

The result can resemble slapstick, except that it is the buyer who is getting it from both ends. In the event of the latter type of agreement, the buyer should attempt to provide some liaison between the vendor's coordinating unit and system testing for both hardware and software. In addition, the buyer should avoid any full payout until there is certification by the coordinating vendor that the full system functions in accordance with (hardware and software) performance specifications. It should be relatively clear that between an OEM and a multi-vendor situation, the former is preferred for accountability and ease of acceptance testing.

A benefit of unit and system testing is the assurance that documentation will be complete, understandable and relatively easy to use. A major failure of most documentation is that it is written by technicians to be understood only by those with similar technical backgrounds. By including training in the acceptance testing period, the buyer's personnel can use the available documentation completely and have the vendor correct any failure to describe functional operations in a readily understandable manner.

Maintenance is the key to product reliability. As previously discussed, reliability is defined as the Up-Time Standard. Failure of the product to perform in accordance with that measure creates a defect. The ability to respond and cure a defect within a particular period of time is critical to maintaining that reliability. For that reason, the buyer should require the vendor to provide: (1) a response time of no more than two hours from receipt of notice that the product is not meeting the Up-Time standard. (An adequate response means the vendor agrees to provide all available resources, within that time frame, reasonably needed to cure any failure of performance); and (2) cure for any failure of performance within a period of time not to exceed one business day. Most vendor agreements use the phrase "best efforts" to describe response and cure-time periods. The argument is that in the event of a persistant problem, the vendor would find itself exposed to liability. The counter argument is that if the vendor is worried about matters beyond its control, it can incorporate a Force Majeure clause in the agreement. (This clause exonerates the vendor from liability for circumstances beyond its control.) A second argument is that recourse would focus on performance. Instead of being liable for liquidated damages or being exposed to litigation, the vendor would be responsible for providing an alternative for processing the buyer's data load (information needed to sustain business operations at that time). This means something other than an alternate site, since if the vendor cannot correct a software defect, then, regardless of where that software is processed, it is going to fail. The answer is that if the vendor cannot restore the Up-Time standard, within the period of time set aside for cure,then a service bureau should be hired by the vendor to process the buyer's data load until such time as cure has been completed. The use of a third party at the vendor's expense would solve the buyer's temporary inability to process business information, thereby motivating the vendor to perform without being punished (by liquidated damages). As in any contract clause, the focus of processing alternatives is on performance, not exposure to liability--making it easier for the vendor to accept. Naturally, some vendors will object, because they want to avoid any payout in the event of a failure to cure. The standard offering is a credit against maintenance fees until such time as the problem is solved. Since a credit doesn't cost the vendor any out-of-pocket money (the monthly maintenance fees are not only retained but payment is continued), there is no incentive for performance. For that reason, a litmus for being responsive is the vendor's willingness to assume responsibility to provide alternative processing in the event it fails to cure the defect.

Liquidated damages are often used by attorneys as a device for motivating vendor response. The concept of such damages is that they reflect an arbitrary sum designed to compensate the buyer for losses suffered due to lack of performance. The problems in applying that concept to maintenance are: (1) money does not equate to performance (The vendor can pay out all the money requested, but if the product doesn't work, the buyer is still stuck); and (2) the liquidated damage amount must equate to the maintenance payments to be considered "compensatory" instead of "punitive." (This means that the specified amounts are relatively low, which reduces the vendor's motivation to perform.) For those reasons, liquidated damages, even if accepted by the vendor, are often self-defeating, creating resistance instead of performance.

Other points to be settled before entering into an agreement should include:

(1) <u>Coverage</u>: The buyer should define the coverage provided by maintenance. Often, if a problem is caused by the buyer's failure to follow operating instructions; or abuse caused by the buyer's personnel; or by power outage, then the vendor will charge an additional cost. To avoid costs relating to instructional problems (how to operate the system), the vendor should provide buyer's personnel with a checklist that must be followed before contacting the vendor. If that checklist is not followed, the vendor would be entitled to an additional fee for curing a problem that ought not to have occurred. If it is followed, then no additional fee should be assessed for requiring the vendor to perform.

Preventive maintenance coverage requires the vendor to tear down the product periodically to perform diagnostics in order to catch potential defects. For software products, such tearing-down is done by vendors at their place of business, on a regular basis. The results (called "fixes") should be provided to users on a regular (no cost) basis. In situations where a combination of hardware and software is being maintained, such tearing-down of the hardware should occur on a regular (once each quarter) basis. In addition, any other maintenance support for hardware should be noted in a log, kept by the buyer, describing the date, time, nature of service call, and how the problem was resolved. This log tends to be particuarly useful in situations involving sloppy maintenance. For example, a third party maintenance repair serviced failed to cure the recurring functional inability of a mainframe. The buyer kept a detailed log of all repair calls and had each entry initialed by the vendor's service representative. The log revealed three different representatives, each duplicating the other's work. The buyer's employees also observed that the vendor's representatives were sloppy in handling component parts (circuit boards), causing a large number to be chipped or cracked, all of which were charged to the buyer. The vendor's bill for parts and time totalled more than $11,000. The buyer objected, and received a letter from the vendor's attorney threatening suit. The buyer sent that attorney a copy of its maintenance log, together with affidavits from several employees who recorded their observations of the vendor representative's material-handling procedures. In addition, that attorney received a demand for $6000 to reimburse the buyer for the costs of hiring a third party maintenance service to cure the problem. Result, the original vendor not only rescinded its bill for $11,000, but agreed to pay a portion of the buyer's $6000 reimbursement demand. Lesson: keep detailed records of all maintenance service activities to avoid being stuck with the high cost of poor service.

Generally, maintenance provided during normal business hours (defined in contract) is covered by the annual maintenance fee. However, it is not unusual to require maintenance service during periods beyond the business day; for that reason, it should be clearly stated that additional (overtime) charges begin only if the maintenance service **begins** after the normal business day. If such service extends beyond that time period, there should be no charge.

Another maintenance service concern is avoidance of interference with the buyer's normal business operations. There is the story of the computerized telephone system that failed to function. To repair the problem, the vendor had to shut down the system, closing the buyer's real estate brokerage business for a week. The system was fixed, but the buyer almost went bankrupt. Solution: in the event of an impairment of the buyer's business caused by extended repair (more than one business day) of the system, the vendor should be obligated to provide an alternative designed to substantially support the buyer's information usage load.

(2) Assignment: The right to sell (assign) receivables (payments) is commonly found in installment sales or lease agreements. This right is important to vendors, because it provides cash flow at a discount. For instance, the vendor sells the right to receive payments from a buyer who purchased a turnkey system on installment. The assignee who purchases that right to receive payments usually pays less than the contract face value (discount). In addition, the assignee expects to be insulated from liability in the event the vendor fails to perform. This expectation is expressed as the "hell or high water clause." In essence, it means that the payments continue regardless of whether the vendor has performed (keep paying, come hell or high water). Courts will uphold the assignment provision as long as the one making the installment payments receives notice that there has been an assignment. Take the case of the rather naive buyer who was mesmerized by the sales pitch for a minicomputer. To clinch that deal, the vendor ("honest Sam") made the buyer an offer he couldn't refuse. Two

contracts were provided. One was a "guarantee" that if the buyer was not satisfied within thirty days, he could get his money back. The second was a standard installment sales agreement that contained the infamous "hell or high water" assignment clause. Neither contract had any language indicating an inter-relationship. Predictably, the buyer called "honest Sam" within that thirty-day period to request that he remove the computer. The response was a recording that the phone number had been disconnected (for non-payment). At that same time, a notice was received from a local bank indicating that it was the assignee for the installment payments due on the contract for that computer. The buyer refused to make payments, indicating that the vendor had breached its first agreement (of which the bank had no knowledge). The court ruled in favor of the bank, indicating that the bank's lack of notice insulated its right to collect payments under the hell or high water clause from any other agreement.

The insulation of assignments has been qualified recently by consumer legislation that gives the buyer a right to void a purchase within a short period of time (three business days). However, that legislation applies to individuals, not businesses that are often not considered "consumers" within the context of that legislation.

The lesson of the hell or high water clause is that the buyer must be certain of the vendor's credibility. It is rare that this clause would ever be excluded from an agreement. For that reason, if the buyer is going to be unable to relate performance to payment (after acceptance), then it must assure such certainty before acceptance.

(3) <u>Limitation</u> <u>of</u> <u>Liability</u>: One of the standard provisions found in virtually every vendor contract is a limitation of damages. Basically, it says that in the event of a failure to perform, the vendor will have no liability for consequential damages, and that its exposure to direct and incidental damages is limited to a substitute remedy (such as repair or replace).

(4) <u>A</u> <u>Reasoned</u> <u>Balance</u>: Most users understand that few vendors would be in business if they insured every transaction. At the same time, the law requires compensation for failure to provide the desired goods or services. As with two competing positions, a balance was struck to preserve a modicum of fairness. The law said that if the product had been completely delivered, then the user's focus should be on performance, not money damages. For that reason, a vendor is able to limit its liability to either repairing or replacing the defective product. However, if the repair or replace remedy fails, then the vendor must

return an agreed upon amount (representing all or a fair portion of the monies paid), or find itself stripped of any protection against consequential damages. This was the ruling in the case of <u>Chatlos</u> <u>vs.</u> <u>NCR</u>. The court found that the user had contracted to buy a certain turnkey system. Although the hardware and software modules were described in the contract, the vendor failed to deliver the key software module. Versions of that module were provided, but they did not function as described in the performance specifications attached to the contract. After almost twelve months of trying to get that module to function, the buyer became frustrated and sued the vendor for breach. The latter used the limitation of liability clause as a shield, arguing that the buyer's recourse was limited to repair or replace. This argument failed when the court found that the repair or replace recourse was useless because (after a reasonable period of time) the vendor could not cure the buyer's problem. This meant that the vendor's recourse failed in its "essential purpose," exposing it to consequential damages. In subsequent cases, vendors have been smart enough to include a money payment in the event of failure of its repair or replace remedy.

(5) <u>A</u> <u>Trade-Off</u>: The Chatlos case was important also because it established another principle underlying the effectiveness of liability limitation clauses. The court

found that because the vendor could not provide a certain software module in good working order, the entire system (hardware and software) was never fully delivered. For that reason, it was held that the limitation of liability clause was inapplicable, because the product (on which that clause was based) did not exist. The principle is that the limitation of liability clause is designed to insulate the vendor for a failure of product performance. If the product does not exist, then there is no basis for that shield, and the vendor is fully exposed to liability. This means that a failure to provide a completed product (one that functions in accordance with its performance specifications) voids the limitation of liability shield.

(6) <u>Form</u> <u>of</u> <u>Appearance</u>: Prominant notice of the limitation of liability clause is required in the contract. This has been refined by the courts to mean that the clause should be separately displayed and not "buried" under a misleading heading. In the <u>Jutta</u> <u>vs.</u> <u>Fireco</u> case, the limitation of liability clause was included in the "Benefits" provision of the contract, which discussed the warranty to repair or replace defective parts. The court held that its inclusion in that provision was misleading, since the buyer would not expect to look for a limitation on liability in a provision marked "Benefits." Lesson: a clear, prominant display separately describing limitation of liability is

required. In addition to prominant display, content is important. The language must be specific, enabling the vendor to describe the types of damages that are to be excluded or limited. The three types of damages generally described within this clause are direct, incidental and consequential. Direct damages are those that directly arise out of a failure to perform contractual obligations. For instance, the failure of a vendor to deliver a new product that had been purchased would be a breach of contract. Direct damages would be the money paid in advance for that product, since that is the loss directly arising out of the vendor's failure to perform. Incidental damages are those costs expended in minimizing the loss caused by that breach. In the same example, to mitigate any further losses, the buyer would lease a similar micro-computer, the cost of which would be incidental to the direct damages suffered by the buyer due to the vendor's breach. Consequential damages are those arising out of the buyer's direct loss due to the vendor's breach. To illustrate, the vendor's failure to deliver the micro-computer impaired the buyer's ability to support its marketing personnel, causing a loss of sales. Those lost sales were a consequence of the vendor's failure to perform, and their value constituted the buyer's consequential damages. A clearer description of how those damage classification forms interrelate is the case of the defective disk drive. An insurance company bought a standalone disk drive unit for its programming division. The disk drive unit was delivered, installed by the vendor and certified as being in good working order. The buyer had a disk containing information, costing about $500,000 to formulate, which was vital to its on-going marketing operations. The disk was placed in the drive, the on-button was pressed and the drive erupted into smoke and flames. What were the buyer's direct, incidental and consequential damages?

(a) The breach was failure to provide a product that would function in accordance with its specifications.

(b) As a direct result of the failure of that product to operate properly the buyer's disk (which it placed on the drive) was destroyed. Therefore, the value of that disk media ($5) was the buyer's direct damages.

(c) As a consequence of the loss of that disk media, the information on it was also lost. Therefore, the buyer's consequential damages was the value of the information ($500,0000 contained on the media which was destroyed by the vendor's failure to provide a product that would function in accordance with its performance specifications. There is often an attempt to include loss of market position (sales) as part of consequential damages. Unless evidence exists that sales were actually lost, courts exclude such speculative claims from the catagory of consequential damages.

(d) To minimize the damage resulting from the loss of information contained on the disk, the buyer had to pay a consultant to restructure that data. The costs of that consultant arose as an incident to the consequential damages suffered by the buyer. Therefore, the buyer's incidental damages are the costs incurred in attempting to minimize the loss of data arising out of the vendor's breach.

In addition to those four different types of damages that a buyer would usually incur, there is another type of damage classification called "special." This is defined as simple negligence (unintentional carelessness.) The law permits the buyer to also exclude that type of damage under the limitation of liability clause.

(7) Exclusion and Limitation: The vendor has the right to exclude certain of those decribed damages, while limiting others. The law indicates that only consequential damages may be excluded, providing the exclusionary language is

specific and is displayed in bold type. In effect, the language would state "CONSEQUENTIAL DAMAGES ARE FULLY EXCLUDED." Often, there is additional language indicating that such damages are excluded, whether or not reasonably foreseeable by the vendor at the time of execution (signing the agreement). The added language does not effectively strengthen that exclusion of consequential damages, but it does make some lawyers feel more comfortable. The exclusion of consequential damages conforms to the courts' view that the vendor is not in business to insure the product. Once the product has been delivered, the buyer's recourse should relate to performance, thereby eliminating the need to pursue consequential damages.

Direct and incidental damages may be limited by trade-offs. For instance, a common trade is the exchange of repair or replace for direct and incidental damages. The vendor promises to repair or replace the product, if it fails, in lieu of paying for direct or incidental damages. This type of trade is, of course, in line with the principle that once the product exists and is fully delivered to the user, the focus of recourse should be performance. The limitation on repair or replace is time. The vendor would have a reasonable period of time to perform. However, if the product still doesn't function at the end of that period of time, then the remedy of repair or replace is said to "fail of its essential purpose" (it doesn't work.) In that case the vendor is wide open to liability (despite its exclusion of consequential damages). It seems that limitation of liability is considered as an integrated arrangement. This means that if the sole remedy fails, the entire clause is voided. It is for that very reason that vendors have added money damages to the remedy of repair or replace; in the event the product still fails then the buyer receives a set amount of damages, preserving the vendor's exclusion of consequential damages. Theory aside, what is a reasonable period of time to repair or replace a product? Depending on circumstances, courts have provided answers ranging from 30 to 90 days. The better method is for the buyer and seller to agree on a reasonable period of time in the contract, eliminating ambiguity and its resulting gnashing of teeth.

(8) <u>Unconscionability</u>: This word has been used to express the ultimate power of the court to void limitation of liability, or the agreement itself, where one party had such an inferior bargaining position that it was compelled to accept a one-sided agreement. It has also been used to void an agreement where one party finds itself "surprised" by the contents (proverbial fine print). Courts are generally reluctant to interfere with commercial transaction. The presumption is that both parties, bargaining at arms length, have concluded an agreement that is mutually satisfactory.

Contradicting that presumption is an expensive effort. Take the case of the automatic incinerator machine that was to help a franchisee become a millionaire. The novice businessman bought the franchise and appropriate equipment from the distributor. Unfortunately, the equipment did not incinerate, and the franchisee was stuck with a lot of garbage. The distributor told the franchisee that the contract made him solely responsible for repairing any problems, and indicated that payments were to continue regardless of whether the franchisee could use the equipment. Not a pleasant situation. The franchisee thought it was unfair to be burdened with fixing the equipment while making payments for it and his business reputation was becoming worthless because the equipment would not function. The contract, of course, was air-tight; written by a lawyer who did a meticulous job of protecting his client's interest. The only problem was that he did too good a job. The court agreed with the franchisee. Apparently, prior to execution, the distributor advised the franchisee that the contract was non-negotiable and had to be signed "as-is." Further, the contract contained various acknowledgements by the franchisee which it didn't understand and which remained unexplained by the distributor at the time of execution. The court concluded that since the franchisee was compelled to execute an agreement it didn't understand, enforcement would be unconscionable. With that, it voided the agreement, found the distributor liable for providing impaired equipment, and awarded the franchisee direct and consequential damages for the losses caused by such impaired equipment. It took several years, a lot of money and effort to reach that conclusion. The franchisee won legally, but actually lost, because its business went bankrupt.

(9) <u>Surprise</u>: Not all such cases are so clearly onerous. There is the major corporation that executed a contract for heavy-duty argicultural equipment. Just prior to delivery, there was an economic downturn and the buyer found itself in a cash flow bind. It refused to take delivery on the basis of language in the contract which it "didn't notice" during execution. Claiming "surprise" the buyer argued that the offending language (limitation of liability) was on the back portion of the agreement, not referenced on the front portion that it signed. The vendor argued that most business contract forms have language on both the front and back. This common trade practice was knowledge that the buyer ought to have been aware of, since it was a sophisticated corporation doing business on an international basis. The court, however, agreed with the buyer, finding that it did not have notice of language on the contract's back and could have been reasonably surprised.

In essence, finding that a contract is onerous requires

a detailed understanding of the circumstances that led up to execution of the agreement. There must be proof that: (a) a party was compelled to sign the agreement without fully understanding its contents; and (b) the agreement is so one sided that it compels that party to accept liability that generally would be another's.

(10) <u>Warranties</u>: A warranty is an unconditional promise, as opposed to a representation, which is qualified by specific requirements.

There are two types of warranties. One is "expressed" in the agreement; the other "implied" by law. This chapter has already described two express warranties: identification of the product and how it functions. If the buyer is acquiring a microcomputer with a CPU, two disk drives, keyboard and monitor, then that description identifies the product components expected to be acquired. If the vendor delivers a typewriter instead, then the product offered does not "conform" to the expressed description of what the buyer intended to acquire. Such "non-conformance" is a breach of the vendor's express warranty that the product delivered will conform to a description of the product that the user intended to acquire. Lesson: an express warranty is created automatically (without use of that heading) through the contract description of the product, its identity and functional specifications. The Chatloss case illustrated the signifcance of the express warranty. The contract expressly identified the components (hardware and software) that the vendor had promised to deliver. Failure to provide a software component (identified in the contract) was cited by the court as breach of the vendor's express warranty, permitting the buyer to void the contract, and exposing the vendor to liability for breach.

In addition to identification and function, there are other express warranties that should be found in an agreement:

(a) Authority and Title: The vendor's right to sell, license or distribute the product. This is particularly important for software products, because of the epidemic of piracy in that industry. Witness the user who was able to buy the license for a software product from a vendor for a below-market price. The vendor's pitch was that the price was a special favor to the buyer because he expected to establish a long-term business relationship. The buyer accepted that story despite the fact that it had never heard of the vendor (who had no other products) before and couldn't foresee any further business relationship. Two months later, the buyer found itself enjoined from using that product because the vendor had no right of distribution. Since there was no contract, the buyer could not prove the vendor actually claimed it had the authority to grant a license of use. Make certain, therefore, that the contract indicates a specific statement that the vendor has the authority to grant a license of use, or as a buyer you could end up paying twice for the same product.

(b) No lien or encumbrance, meaning that the right to use or own the product is not subject to a third party debt. For instance, the purchaser of a "hot" new microcomputer suddenly found himself embroiled in a lawsuit by creditors of the vendor. They claimed that the product was subject to a lien which was not cleared when it was sold to the buyer; for that reason, they petitioned the court to permit seizure of that product unless the buyer paid the outstanding debt (oh yes, the vendor went bankrupt). Result: the buyer ended up paying twice for the same product. Avoid such a circumstance by making certain that the contract expressly declares that the product is not subject to any lien or encumbrance.

(e) New, in accordance with Section 38 (as amended) of the 1954 Internal Revenue Code. This means that the buyer can claim an investment tax credit. This warranty is applicable for hardware and for systems (combinations of hardware and software.) At this point software, by itself, is not considered eligible for investment tax credit, since the buyer does not own the software but only has a license to use it.

(d) No infringement of a United States patent or copyright or misappropriation of a trade secret. This warranty is critically important if the buyer is acquiring software. As said previously, piracy is rife in the software industry. A failure to receive a warranty that the vendor did not infringe or misappropriate a proprietary (ownership) right could expose the buyer to third party claims resulting in tremendous expense, aside from loss of the product. Take the case of the insurance company manager whose friend just happened to develop a new software product that performed general ledger applications similar to those of the insurance company's existing, licensed software product. There were some differences, but the similarity was startling. His friend offered to sell this new product to the insurance company at a "super" low rate. How could the manager refuse? He acquired the product, put it in operation, keyed in all appropriate information, and sent the other product back, stopping the original vendor's periodic license payments. The manager subsequently received an innocuous-sounding letter from the original vendor asking why the license product was returned. The manager (to boost his friend's sales) gladly explained the new product, how it worked, and its low license fee. Within one week, the manager received a second letter, this time from that vendor's counsel ordering him to cease and desist from using that product. This letter accused the manager's friend of infringing on the vendor's U.S. copyright, indicated that action had commenced for a preliminary injunction, and threatened the insurance company with damages for aiding such infringement. Confronting his friend, the manager gained an admission that the vendor's product had been copied. With that information, the insurance company responded, agreeing to cease use of that product and agreeing to fully cooperate with the vendor in its suit against the manager's friend. In spite of that letter and its protestations of innocence, the insurance company subsequently agreed to reimburse the original vendor for legal fees to avoid costly lititgation. Lesson: make certain that the vendor not only warrants against infringement or misappropriation of third party proprietary rights, but agrees that in the event of a claim to: (a) fully indemnify the buyer for any and all costs, loss or expenses incurred as a result of any claim (to include but not limited to reasonable attorneys fees); (b) fully defend the claim against the buyer, in the buyer's name, giving the buyer a right to veto any settlement proposal; and (c) return all monies paid by buyer in the event a judgment (issued by a court) or settlement (agreed upon by the parties) impairs the buyer's access to or use of the product. A warning: many vendors have warranties against infringement of U.S. copyright or patent, but these don't include misappropriate of third party trade secrets (proprietary rights.) Always amend those provisions to include trade secrets within the indeminification protection, since most litigation has centered on piracy of such proprietary rights. Further, vendors also try to limit their liability by requiring buyers to wait until the highest constituted tribunal has issued a ruling. The danger is that the user is exposed to a preliminary injunction (issued by the court assuming initial jurisdiction over the matter) which could impair its right to use that product while exculpating the vendor from liability (until perhaps three years down the road when the litigation has been resolved). Indemnification coverage should occur immediately upon notice of claim regardless of resolution.

(11) <u>Implied</u> <u>Warranties</u>: Implied warranties arise by operation of law, and consist of the implied warranty of (a) merchantability and (b) fitness for paricular purpose.

Merchantability indicates that the product is the same as those of the same or similar nature. It is like the express warranty identifying the product, its components and performance specifications. Generally, this warranty is applicable in situations where the written contract expressly idenfities those characteristics of the product. For instance, with the purchase of an automobile, there is an implied warranty that (a) the particular automobile will function as would any other like make, model, year and similar equipment; and (b) it will look the same as would any other of like make, model, year, and similarly equipped. In purchasing a software product, if there is no description of how the product would function, then the implied warranty of merchantability imposes a standard requiring that product to function as would a like software product.

Fitness For Particular Purpose implies that the product provided by the vendor will be customized to meet the buyer's particular business needs. The underlying assumption is that the vendor (a) fully understands the buyer's business expectations; (b) fully understands the buyer's needs, which must be satisfied to achieve those business expectations;

(c) is an expert in its particular business and understands how to craft a product that will fit the buyer's particular needs; and (d) can be fully relied upon to craft a product that will precisely fit the buyer's particular needs. In essence, the relationship between buyer and vendor within this implied warranty is akin to that of fiduciary and client. There is an enormous degree of trust posited by such reliance--meaning that a failure to perform is not just a simple breach of contract but a violation of a personal trust (akin to a lawyer stealing from a client). This implied warranty is applicable to situations where the vendor is to create or modify a product to meet client needs--a fairly common situation with software vendors.

(12) <u>Disclaimers</u>: Naturally, all implied warranties are disclaimed, as well as those express warranties not stated in the contract. This means that (a) the implied warranties are not available to the buyer; and (b) express warranties are not available unless specifically stated in the contract.

Like the limitation of liability clause, the theory underlying disclaimer of warranties is based on the existence of the product. Where a product exists, the disclaimer of warranties insulates the vendor from errors in performance; where there is no product, the disclaimer is ineffective. In the Chatolos case, the vendor failed to deliver the system described in the contract. For that reason, the court held that the disclaimer of warranties was voided because the product did not exist.

Form of display is also critical if the disclaimer is to be effective. The law requires that the disclaimer be in bold type, prominently displayed and specific. This means that the language must appear as follows: EXCEPT AS OTHERWISE STATED HEREIN ANY AND ALL WARRANTIES, BE THEY EXPRESS OR IMPLIED, IN PARTICULAR THE IMPLIED WARRANTY OF MERCHANTABILITY AND/OR THE IMPLIED WARRANTY OF FITNESS FOR PARTICULAR PURPOSE, ARE DISCLAIMED. If the language fails to specifically mention the two implied warranties, they are not excluded.

(13) <u>Termination</u>: The agreement will naturally terminate after the vendor has performed its obligations. However, the express warranties should continue even after the agreement has ended. This means that two years after the software has been accepted, if a third party claims infringement of a copyright, the vendor is still liable for indemnification. To assure continuance of warranties, language must be included to that effect as an exception to termination.

In the event of a failure to perform, there should be a

right of termination in addition to any other remedies. For instance, if the buyer fails to pay the vendor its money, that is a breach and, in addition to litigation, the vendor would have a right to terminate the agreement (it does no good to continue a relationship that is already ineffective).

In the event of termination for breach, the buyer (assuming it is the injured party) would have a right to the return of any and all monies paid to the vendor. Such right creates a de facto lien on any equipment of products owned by the vendor until there is full re-payment to the buyer. Where the vendor was injured by the buyer's breach, there would be a right to "peaceably " enter upon the buyer's premises and "seize" its product. The emphasis is on "peaceably". If the buyer objects, then the vendor must pursue its remedies through the court, petitioning a judge and getting an order (Writ) which gives the sheriff (or constable) a right to seize the vendor's property still in the buyer's possession. The latter would be liable for all court costs, but since it is probably bankrupt, such liability would be meaningless.

(14) Breach: Failure to perform is breach. This should be clearly defined for the vendor as its obligations in the contract. In particular, product performance should be defined as the Up-Time Standard, referred to in the

acceptance clause. Definition of performance avoids ambiguity, permitting easier resolution of a problem. In the event of breach, beside being liable for return of all monies and giving the buyer a right to terminate, there is also liability for damages, unless the parties agree to arbitration. The latter is a remedy designed to maintain the contractual relationship while resolving disputes in a reasonably quick, inexpensive and equitable manner. Like anything else arbitration can be abused. The buyer should make certain that the site is a reasonable proximity from its principal place of business, and that the arbitrator:

(a) has no relationship to or interest in any of the parties;

(b) has a background qualifying it to understand the parties' business arrangement;

(c) understands how to conduct a hearing fairly;

(d) will keep accurate records of the hearing; and

(e) will present a written statement of reasons underlying its conclusions.

In addition, to avoid wasting time and effort, all

arbitration must be defined as binding! The only time a court can overturn an arbitrated decision is if it finds that decision to be capricious (totally unreasonable, based on the facts). Courts seldom overturn an arbitrator's decision, so basically, if arbitration is the method chosen to resolve disputes, then both sides ought to realize that they will be bound by the arbitrator's findings.

(15) <u>Waiver</u>: In the event that a party decides, temporarily, to avoid enforcing a contractual right, or to modify the agreement, the waiver provision permits either such action without permanent loss of that right. For instance, suppose the buyer decides it wants the vendor to modify the functional specifications for the software product. Theoretically, any modification would be outside the contract (warranties and representations of performance), since the buyer's expectations are described by the unmodified functional specifications. This means the vendor (a) does not have to make the modificiations; or (b) if the modifications are made, they will be outside the contractual provisions assuring performance. Both parties would sign a separate document (waiver) modifying the agreement by permitting the vendor to change the existing functional specifications without damaging the buyer's contractual protection of performance or denying the vendor additional payment. The buyer does not lose its assurance of

performance, the vendor does not lose the right to claim additional payment, and the buyer's expectations are satisfied. Temporary non-enforcment of contractual rights works the same way. Illustrative of this is the vendor who could not cure a software problem with a system it was attempting to install. The cure period had elapsed, but the vendor had pleaded for more time. The buyer (being of warm heart and good cheer) orally told the vendor to continue working until it had solved the problem. Meanwhile (since all monies were due on installation) full payment had been made for the system, even though it did not perform in accordance with functional specifications. Another thirty days elapsed, and the buyer's good cheer evaporated in the heat of frustration. Demanding its money back, the buyer told the vendor to take the system and walk. The vendor responded that the buyer had waived any right to reject and was stuck with the system. The court backed the vendor. Lesson: in the event that a party requests non-enforcement of a standard issue, a written document stating that non-enforcement is temporary and subject to the waiving party's right to institute at its discretion.

(16) <u>Taxes</u>: One of the bugaboos of software contracts is that of who pays the personal property taxes on the product. Sales or use taxes are legitimately passed along to the buyer. But personal property taxes reflect ownership

that is vested in the vendor, so why should they be paid by the user? As a way of avoiding that question, vendors build those taxes into the license fee, but freqently, because states have issued legislation specifically taxing software, the buyer is directly confronted with that liability. The issue is often negotiable, depending on who has leverage. Another method of resolution is to study the legislation, which may exempt certain types of software. There is no one answer. To avoid this unfair liability, the buyer is going to have to negotiate with the vendor on this issue.

K.   SUMMARY: THE CONTRACT PROCESS

A software contract reflects the system for creating, implementing and assuring performance of the product. It is not enough to know which are the "right" clauses; the document must reflect the flow of events building a context within which expectations will be achieved. Illustrative is the systems contract which is a combination of hardware and software. Such software often has to be modified to meet accurately the buyer's performance requisites. To understand how to construct the flow of events, we will walk through a typical systems contract:

> (1) Introduction--building a context: The beginning of the contract identifies the parties--who they are, where they're located (principal place of

business), and the date the contract has been signed.

(a) "Whereas" clauses then detail the history of the transaction. It is critically important that these clauses state: (i) the buyer's desire for a system that performs certain functions; (ii) the vendor's representation that it has the expertise to provide a system that meets the buyer's functional expectations; (iii) the buyer's preparation and delivery to the vendor of an RFP that describes the former's business expectations (RFP often designated as a particular exhibit and incorporated by this reference into the contract). Being incorporated into the contract makes the exhibit (RFP) part of the contractual document; (iv) the vendor's receipt of the RFP and delivery to the buyer of a Proposal outlining the solution to the buyer's technical problem (like the RFP, the Proposal is also designated as a particular exhibit and incorporated by reference into this contract); and (v) the buyer's reliance on the vendor to provide the technical solution described in its Proposal.

(b) The concluding clause begins "Now Therefore" and indicates that, based on the above history and the subsequent mutual covenants, the parties have agreed to the terms and conditions contained in the particular agreement. This clause indicates that the preceding events formed a context within which the mutual promises were created.

The importance of the Introduction, aside from identifying the parties, is that it provides an understanding of the intent which underlies the performance expected from the vendor. In the event of litigation, it is that "intent" which often determines the final judgement. In addition, it established "single vendor" responsibility for coordinating the creation and implementation of the system.

(2) <u>Describing the System Package</u>: This provision identifies the hardware and software components of the system. Those components are identified in separate schedules (one labeled hardware and another software) that are attached to the agreement. The software schedule will indicate the unmodified programs, those that are modified, and any that are to be created for the buyer. Collectively those hardware and software components should be defined as the "System."

(3) <u>Creating the Functional Specifications</u>: The vendor is to deliver existing and new functional specifications to the buyer within a specified period of time. The vendor should also promise that those functional specifications will conform to the buyer's expectations as reflected in the RFP.

Delivery will not be complete until the buyer receives the narrative for each software module, which includes a description of the internal methodology (its logic and syntax) as well as the data files (layout and screen), the sequence of processing, and disk file organization. This narrative contains the description of the software's functional specifications. The document should be identified as a separate schedule and incorporated by reference into the agreement.

Response/inquiry time should be defined as part of the functional specifications. This standard for generating a response from the system (regardless of the application being performed) should be within the range of two to four seconds, with any exceptions noted by the vendor in the functional specifications.

The combination of narrative and response/inquiry time frame constitutes the software's performance specifications.

(4) <u>Purchase Price Payment</u>: Purchase price should be paid installments tied to performance. For instance: 10% on execution of the agreement; 15% upon completing delivery of the software functional specification; 25% upon completing off-site testing of the sytem; and the remainder upon acceptance. The objective is to hold back the vendor's profit until the system has been thoroughly tested, and proves that it can function in

accordance with its performance specifications. There is no greater leverage than money to motivate performance.

(5) <u>Leverage</u> <u>Grant</u>: This generally indicates an irrevocable, non-exclusive, non-assignable, and non-transferable license provided to the buyer for use of the software product in accordance with the agreement. This license grant means that the buyer has only "a right of use," which cannot be given to any other person or entity (whether subsidiary or creditor). In effect, the license grant is a personal right, which reverts back to the vendor if the buyer no longer exists or breaches the duty of care covenants contained in the agreement.

Restrictions on license use, as discussed in Chapter 3 of this book, are identified in this clause. The objective is to create a "duty of care" in which the buyer is bound to protect the integrity of the software under pain of extensive liability.

Also appearing here is a statement of confidentiality, in which the buyer acknowledges that a direct and confidential relationship exists between it and the vendor for use of the software. This is important because it lays the basis for classifying the software as a "trade secret" of the vendor, adding to the buyer's potential liability for breach of restrictions on use and access.

(6) <u>Warranties</u>: Aside from title, authority, investment tax credit, quiet enjoyment (no liens or encumbrances), performance standards, and non-infringement of a U.S. patent or copyright or misappropriation of a trade secret the vendor also warrants that it will pass through to the buyer the hardware manufacturer's warranties.

The warranties will be deemed "continuing,"surviving termination of the agreement. This means that after the vendor has completed its performance, the obligations it assumed (through those warranties) will continue. Illustrative is the example of a buyer who, two years after it acquired a software product, found itself embroiled in a suit for infringement of copyright. Even though the transaction had been completed, the vendor was bound to honor its indemnification obligations contained in the warranty of non-infringment.

Although often called a "warranty," the repair or replace remedy for failure of the product to perform will be included in this section. It is important for the buyer to incorporate a standard of performance (Up-Time Standard) and time limits for employing that remedy in order to avoid ambiguity. This means that if there is a failure of the product to meet the Up-Time standard during the warranty period, the vendor will have a limited period of time to employ its repair or replace remedy or find itself liable for breach.

The disclaimer clause will be displayed in bold type. It is important that the buyer list all express warranties in the contract.

(7) <u>Implementation Process</u>: This is the heart of the contract. It lays out the steps for:

(i) Creating and delivering the functional specifications;

(ii) Drawing the program code;

(iii) Off-site unit and system testing;

(iv) Delivery of hardware;

(v) On-site unit and system testing, as well as training of employees; and

(iv) Acceptance.

These steps, as previously described in this chapter, should be detailed so that no ambiguity exists.

This section is important because it describes the systematic process in which the components of the product are created, combined, delivered, and tested and proven, functional in an integrated and compatible manner. Again, a contract is not just a series of independent clauses, but the description of a project plan for creating a system that meets the buyer's particular needs. For that reason, each of the implementation steps (described in this section) should be bounded by specific time parameters so there can be no ambiguity regarding levels of performance.

(8) <u>Maintenance</u>: This should focus on "single vendor" responsibility. This means that one vendor should be responsible for maintaining the entire system (both hardware and software). Response and cure-time periods should be detailed, as well as contingencies in the event of failure. In addition, the maintenance fee, initial term (when it begins and duration), as well as non-business hour maintenance charges should be detailed. The contingencies available in the event that there is a failure to cure should also be described (repeating the description of alternatives found in the repair or replace clause of the warranty section.) Finally, the vendor should promise not to interfere with the buyer's business operations while providing maintenance service. This last clause is important because it could prevent a buyer from having to choose between the shutdown of its business or the offer of maintenance service.

(9) <u>Limitation</u> <u>of</u> <u>Liability</u>: This basically protects the

vendor.   To be effective, it must meet the requisites described in this Chapter.

(10) <u>Notice</u>: This is a clause that describes the method by which the parties will communicate, as well as the individuals authorized by the respective parties to receive such communication.

(11) <u>Breach</u> <u>and</u> <u>Termination</u>:   This clause defines a "failure to perform," the alternative remedies available for such failure, and the right of an injured party to terminate the agreement without liability. Arbitration is often included in this section, allowing the parties to resolve the breach without resorting to litigation, while maintaining the contractual relationship.

(12) <u>Waiver</u>: This permits a party to modify the agreement or temporarily excuse an obligation without permanently damaging its contractual rights.

(13) <u>Jurisdiction</u>: This clause establishes the law of a particular state as that which controls resolution of disputes. The dangerous part of this clause is the "venue" section, which indicates that litigation will occur in a particular county in that designated state. The result could be that it would be too expensive for the buyer to pursue its remedies in court.

(14) <u>Authority</u>:   This means that the parties who execute the contract have the right to bind their respective principals.

(15) <u>Integration</u>:   This clause indicates that all prior agreements are superseded and merged into the contract.   This means that, unless specifically identified in the contract, any prior or contemporaneous, oral or written agreements, are worthless.   So the friendly vendor representative's side letter, which is not referenced in the agreement, is not worth the paper it is printed on.   That is why all those exhibits and schedules are identified and made part of the agreement: so that the expectations expressed in those documents are made part of the contract.

There are other "boilerplate" clauses that may be included in a contract.   Those cited above are the basic provisions that most buyers should understand.

Final Note: It is critical that an agreement: (1) be easily understood by both parties; (2) reflect accurately the reality of the transaction; (3) create a system for orderly implementation so that the buyer can easily administer the vendor's obligations; and (4) provide recourse that focuses on performance, permitting a quick and inexpensive resolution of disputes or failures. (The "Art of Negotiating" is discussed in Chapter 5.)

NOTES

CHAPTER III

PRESERVING OWNERSHIP

A. THE OVERALL PROBLEM

The new gold is software! Those rushing to claim its riches have fueled an industry worth over $15 billion. Like the western gold rush, the fight to draw property lines--fencing off products and ideas--has spawned a cast of characters stranger than fiction. It has also changed existing forms of proprietary protection, resulting in laws and concepts that have revolutionized the legal landscape. This Chapter will delve into the twists and turns of protecting innovation (preserving ownership).

The fragility of the ideas and logic underlying software can best be understood through comprehension of how software is created. A "flow chart" is a graphical representation of the set of commands used to instruct the computer. The fundmental idea for those intructions is mathematical--an algorithm capable of being represented by different symbols (zeros and ones). This flow chart is then translated into an alphanumeric form called "source doe" derived from any one of several "computer languages" such as "C" Cobol, Basic, Pascal, or Fortran. Next, an "assembly program" is constructed which translates the source doe into a mechanically readable computer language known as "object code."

Unlike the source code, that can be read by a trained programmer, only a computer can read the assembly program or object code.

The uninitiated should know that there are two major types of software: application and operation. Application programs instruct the computer how to process the raw data. Word processing, number crunching (spreadsheet analysis), etc.-- comprise the bulk of software products and are the programs that perform the "applications" for which the computer was acquired. Operating programs instruct the computer how to process the application programs. This program is often an integral part of the computer hardware (frequently contained on a chip) and is sold as part of the computer equipment. One such program was the basis for the suit brought by Apple against Franklin. The suit will be discussed later in this book.

Defining or establishing ownership of software technology revolves around the problem concerning how to stake out property lines in the user's mind. Like the ancient explorers who hoisted flags in the new world, vendors have learned to put "flags" of ownership on software products to protect their markets. The weakness here is that the user has to be made to believe that the software is owned by a particular vendor, and not by himself. That belief is often difficult to create, regardless of the number or size of "flags" used.

The importance of ownership is found in economics of the market. A total of $15 billion in software sales is projected for 1984. That figure produces a tremendous incentive to "own" a piece of the action. Like the old west, claim-jumping (called software piracy) has become a common practice. That practice of taking someone else's product and putting another brand on it is creating all the turmoil that is producing lawsuits, criminal liability, and modification of existing laws.

Adding to this tendency to claim jump is the volatility of the software market. Idea-oriented products produce dollars until the idea is lost or surpassed. Unauthorized public disclosure therefore means the loss of competitive edge, and that translates into lost dollars (zero market). Worse, if a competitor improves upon the idea, a new market for the better product is created. One would think that the easiest way to protect an idea would be to lock it in a vault. True, but how, then, is it to be marketed? You can't sell something that can't be demonstrated, so the vendor is in a dilemma. To capture a good share of the market, the product must be advertised, exposing the product's basic ideas to competition. At the same time, new markets may be lost, because the competition may improve upon the idea, creating a better product, and so on. This equation yields volatile, rich dynamic and pressure conscious market where ideas produce big dollars that can vanish overnight--hence, the pressure to preserve those ideas without inhibiting the ability to market.

Illustrative of this type of dilemma is a software product developed for CAD/CAM engineering. It was a graphic-oriented product that would permit the engineer to design and stress-test all the elements of a new product on a computer--a breakthrough worth millions. No longer would manufacturers have to build expensive mock-ups and do "seat-of-the-pants" stress testing. The engineering organization that created the product wanted a prototype on the market as soon as possible in order to begin advance sales. Management's idea was to quickly recoup costs by creating an immediate market. To accomplish this, breakfast meetings were held with the engineers of leading manufacturers, where in-depth demonstrations and discussions, and detailed literature were used to promote the product's performance features. A market was created. Management was successful. Costs were being recovered and sales were growing. Then disaster struck. An engineer instrumental in the product's development left and created a slightly better version. The market, so carefully created and nurtured by the original vendor, was lost. Allegations of theft and unfair competition were lodged against the new vendor and its employee. A lawsuit was initiated, but all efforts to thwart the competition failed. The court concluded that the ex-employee-competitor did not steal anything, because there was no secret to steal. By trying to make a market, the original vendor compromised any hope of preserving

146

the product's secret nature. Indeed, through in depth discussion, demonstrations, and literature, freely given to anyone showing a modicum of interest, any vestige of secrecy was lost. The predicament was clear: how could management market a "secret" product without compromising its "secret nature"?

Vendors are not alone in worrying about the loss of secrecy. Users of software products are often exposed to tremendous liability due to breach of license restrictions. As noted in Chapter 2 license restrictions are designed to preserve the vendor's market by inhibiting access, copying, and distribution. "Breach" means that the user has failed to preserve confidentiality, thereby exposing the product's secret. One would think that it is rather easy to obey clear-cut prohibitions. Unfortunately, those restrictions are often drafted poorly (leading to confusion), or ignored by the technical employees hired to operate the product.

Consider the drug company mentioned in Chapter 2, whose employee wrongfully disclosed a licensed software product. The vendor's license contract was signed in good faith, with the drug company pledging to obey restrictions on use and access. The employee acted in good faith, but was curious about how the licensed product operated. Result: a $6 million dollar lawsuit, settled for a six figure number. The user's dilemma: how to protect itself from curious employees who might cost millions in consequential damages.

The risk of loss confronting vendors and users is the prime motivator for developing devices used to protect innovative ideas and products.

B. TRADE SECRET PERSERVATION

The trade secret is the foremost of all proprietary devices. It protects ownership of the idea and the manner in which it is manifested through contractual arrangement that restrict use and access. The type of idea and product protected must be conducive to sales and increased revenue--providing, in essence, a competitive edge. The trade secret must be developed through an investment of time, money, and effort. It must be designed so that its use provides a business advantage over the competition. Finally, the product must be restricted from the general public, and treated as a secret, so only those who have authorized access can obtain its benefits.

With such a broad definition, virtually any idea from can openers to sealing wax can be a trade secret. In fact, the types of trade secret devices are varied, and include perfumes, softdrinks, flavorings, customer lists, electronic circuit masks for silicon chips, etc.

Saying it is a secret and keeping it one are two very different matters. Take the ring manufacturer who created a computer software product to control the molding of rings. The formula was labelled as a trade secret; but the employee who created it signed no confidentiality statement, and the software product was not listed as a secret on any documents signed by employees who later terminated their relationship with the manufacturer. A key employee (who helped create the software product) left the manufacturer to work for a competitor. A similar software program for computerized ring molding was created by the competitor. The original manufacturer sued, arguing theft of a trade secret by its key employee. Believing it had an open and shut case, the developing company rejected all forms of settlement. After all, the particular employee created the product, admittedly took the ideas for that product with him, and used them for a competitor's benefit. The decision however, favored the employee. How was that possible? The answer: the ring manufacturer failed to preserve the software product's secret nature, in that the company did not:

Limit access to essential employees only. (In fact, virtually every employee from janitor to president had access.)

Require all employees who might have access to sign confidentiality statements, listing that product as a trade secret.

Audit access to preserve its "secret" nature against unauthorized usage.

In reality, even though the software product was described as a "secret" the ring manufacturer failed to limit use and access, thereby losing the right to maintain proprietary interest.

Clearly, saying is different than doing. Courts require that the owner enforce the "secrecy" of a software product to preserve exclusive rights of ownership. How and to what extent secrecy measures are taken often spells the difference between maintaining a competitive edge and losing a dream.

Day-to-day treatment of the software program is the key to protecting a trade secret.

1. Confidentiality Covenants, signed by all individuals who use or access those "trade secret" programs, are necessary. For example, the employer should require employees to acknowledge in writing that certain software products (to be subsequently identified) are proprietary and considered "secret." Identification consists of a listing that is changed in the course of employement. Confidentiality Covenants provide a basis for identifying "secret" products.

The problem with Confidentiality Covenants is that they are drawn by lawyers who have no concept of the employer's business needs or the employee's need to understand the document. Often those documents read like a deed written by a scribe whose model was the Declaration of Independence. A good illustration is the entire data processing division of an insurance company that had the good sense to refuse to sign a Confidentiality Covenant drawn by the in-house real estate attorney. The document contained intimidating language and threats, and had no statement of reasons to indicate why confidentiality was important. Needless to say, that document was hurriedly rewritten.

To be effective, a Confidentiality Covenant must be clear, specific, and understandable--or it will be voided by courts as ambiguous. It must also be specific--identifying (by name, number or code) all the particular confidential items accessed by the employee. Losing a multi-million dollar product just because of an unelaborated phrase that said "all software products are considered a trade secret" is not fun. Courts require specificity, and if that's not possible then at least descriptions of the type of products involved must be included. Otherwise, there is ambiguity and the Confidentiality Covenant wouldn't be worth the paper on which it's written.

Another concern besides clarity and specificity is the type of individual who executes that document. It should be a key employee. Having everyone from janitor to president execute the same Confidentiality Covenant creates an assumption of universal access. This creates the inverse assumption that the product is general knowledge and not a "secret." Pinpointing individuals gives a company the opportunity to prove that the software is a secret because access is restricted. There is an infamous case of an employer who actually made everyone from janitor to president sign the same Confidentiality Covenant which listed items considered proprietary and confidential. When a sales representative took a customer list and was sued, the employer found the Confidentialtiy Covenant ineffective proof that the sales representative had stolen a "secret." The court ruled that the document proved nothing except equal access to the software product. Make the documents special. Have only those employees with a "need to know" sign the Confidentiality covenant.

Restrictive covenants are often included in confidentiality documents. They restrict an employee from competing with the employer in the same line of business, for a specific period of time, within a particular geographic area. The language often prohibits those employees from soliciting--for a certain period after termination--the employer's customers (or even potential customers) with whom the employee has had contact. The whole purpose of such covenants is to intimidate key employees and prevent them from competing in the same market. Unfortunately, the language is often so restrictive in terms of time and geography that those covenants are generally voided by courts. Even if the language is "reasonable" (whatever that means), courts are reluctant to enforce restrictive documents because the result would be an involuntary servitude (violating the 13th Amendment). In essence, the courts view those covenants as depriving a person of the right to earn a livelihood without just compensation. There are, however, exceptions to every rule. An example is the sales representative who signed a confidentiality covenant containing a restriction against competing with the employer in the same geographic area (defined as the continental United States) for a period of one year after termination of employment. This document, however, also pledged the employer to pay the sales representative his base salary for that period of time providing the restriction was satisfied. As can be predicted, the employee left, went to work for a competitor within the geographical area described in that document, and found himself facing a lawsuit. The court upheld the restrictive covenant because the sales representative was not denied a livelihood. Indeed, the base salary received for not competing was deemed to be generous by the standards of that industry; therefore, payment of a salary for upholding the "non-compete" restriction results in enforceble obligations on the employee.

A second exception to the courts' negative view of restrictive covenants concerns solicitaton of current customers. Often the restrictive covenant is limited in scope, prohibiting the ex-employee, for a period of six months after termination, from soliciting the employer's current customers (with whom the employee has had contact). The courts have found such a restriction to be reasonable, since the employee is not deprived of the right to identify his own customers and compete in the market with his former employer. However, as with all good things, there are limits. Employers often add the phrase "potential customers" to the restriction. This is a highly ambiguous term and is not likely to be upheld by any court. Also it can be frustrated by the ex-employee who needs only a document from the customer indicating that it does not believe itself to be (at the time of the ex-employee's solicitation) a potential customer of the former employer. Such a document would undercut any attempt by the employer to prove a violation of that restrictive condition.

So a confidentiality covenant would be enforceable if it is written in an undertstandable manner and limited to key employees. Further, the restrictive covenant portion of such a document would be upheld if, (1) the employee is compensated for loss of livelihood or (2) is limited to soliciting current customers, contacted during employment, and (3) for a period not to exceed six months.

(2) <u>Work Rules</u> that establish standards of behavior affecting access to confidential products and information are another requirement for trade secret protection. It does no good to have everyone sign a well-drawn confidentiality covenant and then to permit unrestrained, universal access to proprietary products. Witness the New York City Department of Education, which tried to fire a programmer who continually used the mainframe computer to trace geneology of race horses. Obviously, satisfying a penchant for the ponies would not be within this individual's job description. However, such activity was condoned for a long period of time in spite of specific work rules to the contrary. Any existing work rules were unenforced, and the employee continued to use the mainframe to pursue his fantasy. Unfortunately, a new supervisor discovered the activity, was distressed and fired the employee. Upset at being fired, and possibly losing access to his gambling edge, he sued to get his job back. One would think that he would have as much change as the proverbial snowball in that place where the sun doesn't shine. Well, they would be wrong! The employee won, because the Department of Education could not provide it had enforceable work rules governing employee behavior. Indeed, the

court found that the permitted standard of behavior was "anything goes." Access to facilities and proprietary products was universal and unrestricted. In such circumstance, the employer could not arbitrarily change the permitted standard of behavior without reasonable notice. So the lesson is clear. Create work rules, enforce them, and document the enforcement.

Only by showing restricted access to certain information can the employer prove that information is "special" and thereby "secret."

Examples of work rules would be those that:

-- Specify that source code listing be available only to certain employees having need to know.

-- Use password systems to limit access to certain files.

-- Require the locking of proprietary information in designated files, safes or containers after work has been completed.

-- Establish lines of communication permitting supervisory personnel to control work in progress.

156

-- Require that the restricted areas be limited to certain personnel.

In addition to work rules, physical security should be employed, using badges and magnetic codes to enhance the employer's argument of limited access.

An important part of the work environment is dialogue with employees to avoid problems that might lead to computer abuse or sloppy performance. Informal discussions on the nature and importance of proprietary information can go a long way toward convincing a technician not to "hack around." However, those discussions should be meaningful to the employee, not just a gimmick used by management to "keep the natives happy." Illustrative is the saga of a vice president who, with much fanfare, initiated small informal employee discussion groups. After the first two weeks, it was evident that the vice president was using employees to build his ego instead of their morale. The resulting disillusionment caused a fall in work quality greater than previously experienced. "Blue flu" and sloppiness were so endemic to the operation that the entire data processing division virtually collapsed into a mass of endless bickering. Avoiding that situation requires a sensitivity by management toward the employees' need to receive honest feedback and see progress in bettering the work environment.

In essence, work rules are important to establish proof that certain information and software products are not only proprietary but confidential. Such rules must be published in a concise and understandable form. They should be enforced on a fair and consistant basis, with allowance for employee feedback.

(3). <u>Top</u> <u>Management</u> <u>commitment</u> to preserving the "secret" nature of proprietary data is needed. Such a commitment, published in the form of a clear and concise policy statement, indicates that resources have been committed to preserving a proprietary interest in confidential information or software products. This policy statement should be published, incorporated in employee orientation material, and used as the basis for requiring Confidentiality Covenants and work rules.

Physical security, the use of a Policy Statement, a Confidentiality Covenant and Work Rules, gives an employer an integrated proprietary protection program for assuring the "secret" nature of proprietary products. One could rely on an integrated proprietary protection program to create a standard of behavior permitting it to control employee behavior and establish a recognized standard of due care. The latter is important because it shields the user of licensed software products from liability in the event suit is brought by a licensor for breach of its license (contract) restrictions. Illustrative is the insurance company that was sued by a software vendor because the insurer's employee had wrongfully copied and then tried to seal (with some minor modifications) a software product licensed under contract to the insurer. The employee was fired and sued by the insurer to recover any losses incurred. The software vendor claimed its competitive edge was lost, sued for millions and then was stopped short when its own lawyers found that the contract with the insurance company contained an acknowledgement that the insurer's integrated proprietary protection program was an acceptable level of due care. Result, the insurer was saved from a costly lawsuit through a standard of due care that effectively regulated employee access and distribution of third party proprietary products. Vendors and users can both use such an integrated proprietary protection program to identify and preserve trade secrets against employee theft.

But consider the marketing dilemma. How does a vendor protect itself from losing the "secret" nature of its products? To answer that question requires an understanding of the advantages and disadvantages of the concept known as "trade secret." This proprietary device protects the idea and the manner in which it has been expressed. For instance, the idea underlying a software program is protected as well as the logic and syntax used by that program to convey the idea. Only patent protection is as strong in terms of what it protects. The weakness of trade secret protection is "disclosure." A trade secret can be lost through independant discovery, innocent access, or reverse engineering. For instance, a manufacturer of dental powder believed that the product was a trade secret because it was composed of a unique combination of publicly known elements. Acting to protect this "secret," it licensed distributers, had employees sign confidentiality statements and generally restricted use and access. A competitor suddenly appeared with a substantially similar formula. Believing that its "secret" had been stolen, the manufacturer sued. Records showed that the competitor admitted that the product was identical but claimed discovery through reverse engineering. In essence, the competitor had bought the manufacturer's product, broke down its elements and discovered their unique combination. The court found that the competitor's action was not theft and dismissed the manufacturer's lawsuit. So reverse engineering is a valid method of "discovering" another's trade secret.

Another valid way of "discovering" a trade secret is innocent access. An example of that situation involves a programmer who wrongfully copied and then modified his employer's "secret" code for a new software product. The programmer then sold the "secret" to another individual who used it to create the very product being marketed by the programmer's employer. Imagine the anger of the employer as it found its market usurped by a competitor. Suit was brought and the products were admitted by the competitor to be identical. However, it argued that the "secret's" purchase was made in good faith without any knowledge that the code was stolen. Case closed! There was no theft by the competitor, leaving the original owner with little hope of regaining its market advantage, or even being compensated for its loss.

As indicated, the problem of trade secret disclosure is caused by: independent discovery, reverse engineering, unauthorized access, or innocent access. Once disclosed, by whatever methods, the "secret" is gone. Accordingly, for successful marketing of trade secret products follow three rules: be careful, very careful, and extremely careful!

The methods used to protect and market trade secret software products consist of:

Notice: For what it is worth, language is placed on the product (or programmed in the software code) declaring that it is a trade secret, owned by the author, distributed only by the licensed market organization and that its use is restricted to licensed

161

individuals. Notice is important because it is the first step in proving that a third party knew the product was someone else's trade secret. Remember the problem of innocent access. No third party can make that claim if the product itself states clearly and unequivocably that it is a trade secret belonging to a particular vendor, and that no one, except authorized parties, is permitted access.

Limited Demonstration: Marketing personnel often either provide demonstrations of how the software product functions or issue marketing information describing the product's features. If the demonstration or marketing material is too limited the product will not create a market (will not attract sufficient interest). If, however, the demonstration or material is too generous (as with the CAD/CAM software), those viewing or reading will have an opportunity to "reverse engineer." This poses a dilemma of delicate proportion. By coming on with confidentiality statements, warnings and other legal bugaboos, potential buyers will be "turned off." By not indicating any restrictions the "secret" could be lost. Such a loss occurred to a software author who demonstrated his product to a distributing company. Believing in the good faith of the friendly vice president, the author gave an in-depth presentation, permitting notes, and then left the product with the distributor for "review." True, the distributor did not copy that product. Instead, it "reverse engineered," creating a similar but slightly different version. Oh yes, the author received a note thanking him for his cooperation but "rejecting" his product.

How can we resolve this dilemma without inhibiting the ability to create a market? First those invited to the demonstrations should be limited in number. Second, no notes of any kind should be permitted; instead each attendee should receive a general descripton of the product's functional performance. Third, any independant analysis should be discouraged; instead, the author should provide a money-back warranty for a period of time if the product fails to perform. In this way, the product can be demonstrated effectively, creating a market, without fear of reverse engineering. Market literature should also be general, focusing on functions performed, not on how performance occurs. One of the key problems burdening software vendors is that their literature is often written by engineers who disclose more than necessary. But what about the major sale, where the buyer wants his data processing personnel to analyze the product to determine not only how it works but whether it is appropriate for his business needs? Again, reliance should be placed on a contract containing:

Confidentiality language restricting access to certain employees with a need to know, use of the product solely for analysis, and permitting access for a short (specifically stated) period of time. In addition, copying should be prohibited as well as removal from the specified site. The customer should be required to return any and all notes to the vendor along with the product after the review period has been terminated.

A presumption of theft if any similar product is developed by the customer, or with its assistance, for a period of six (6) months after analysis has been completed. This admission forecloses any argument for reverse engineering.

An audit provision giving the vendor a right to audit the customer's data processing shop within a certain period of time after the analysis has been completed, to make certain no copies have been retained. This puts the customer on notice that any activity other than analysis would be discoverable.

Such a contract makes theft or reverse engineering an unacceptable risk. Suppose, however, the customer balks and doesn't want to sign such a contract. As they say about suspicion, if it walks like a duck, feels like a duck and looks like a duck, go somewhere else!

<u>License</u> <u>Agreements</u>: Use of any trade secret must be controlled to avoid loss through "public distribution." A trade secret retains its "secret" characteristic if distribution occurs on a limited basis to authorized users. For that reason, a license agreement is employed to identify the limited group of users and describe restrictions designed to inhibit theft, loss of revenue or unauthorized disclosure. Like any contract, a license agreement should be specific, clear, concise and easy to administer. A software vendor does not benefit if users cannot understand the agreement. For instance, a software vendor licensed an insurance company to use a particular product. Unfortunately, the agreement encompassed several different types of products, and the vendor failed to designate clearly which product was specifically covered. In addition the restrictions on use and access varied according to the particular product being

licensed. As a result, since the product was never clearly designated, the appropriate restrictions were not defined and the vendor had no contractual basis to prevent public distribution of its "secret" product.

Often, as in any contractual arrangement, modifications occur. Obviously, they should be in writing and should specify which sections of the agreement are being changed, deleted or amplified. In one situation, reminiscent of a bad B grade movie, the attorneys for both a software vendor and a user failed to indicate which sections of the vendor's contract were changed by an addendum. Result: lawsuit to correct a problem that should never have occured. To adapt what is sometimes said about war and generals, law is too important to be left to lawyers. Read the document carefully, make sure it is understandable and be certain that it fully reflects expectations, before signing on the dotted line.

The basic provisions of a software license agreement are described in Chapter II. Suffice it to say that maintaining a "secret" requires limited distribution to selected individuals, with that distribution shown only through a licensing arrangement. For that reason, trade secret devices have been used generally with individuals, not with mass market transactions. Lately, however, courts have indicated that a trade secret is not pre-empted (terminated) by copyright notice appearing on the same product, providing there is proof of limited (non-public) distribution. This means that mass-marketed software products, "licensed" (not generally distributed) to end-users and bearing copyright notice, may also be protected by a trade secret. The effect is to circumvent any vestige of contractual equanimity. The user is compelled to accept the restrictions on use and access regardless of the reality of its environment. The result is that, like paying taxes, people look for a way out. This often means ignoring those restrictions by making unauthorized copies, thereby reducing respect for legal requirements and leading to more abuse of proprietary interests. In a way, it is the proverbial vicious circle: the more vendors try to use one-sided (virtually non-negotiable) contractual arrangements, the more users tend to ignore prohibitions, weakening the very proprietary interest which the vendor has attempted to protect. A better way might be to recognize reality and treat mass-marketed software like phonograph records, selling them at a price that makes copying uneconomical.

(4) <u>Enforcement</u>: In general, a license arrangement is the only way to prove the limited distribution necessary to show the product's "secret nature." Unbelievably, after the software vendor has gone through a license arrangement, the contractual restrictions are generally unenforced. After execution, the software vendor is so concerned with marketing that it forgets to monitor its contractual restrictions limiting use and access. The software training methodology licensed to a major financial institution illustrates this. The contract contained the expected restrictions on use and access, as well as audit provisions that gave the vendor a right to periodically audit the user's manner of protecting the methodology's integrity. After six (6) years of not even inquiring if the methodology was being used, let alone protected from disclosure, the vendor walked into a user's data processing shop, without notice, and demanded the right to audit. Counsel for the institution demanded that the vendor leave and, subsequently, the user advised the vendor that it had waived its audit rights through non-use of these rights. Although the vendor was eventually satisfied with a letter indicating that contractual restrictions were being maintained, the lesson of waiver through non-use remains clear. If a right has to be enforced by the vendor, non-enforcement for long periods of time creates an assumption, which can be reasonably relied upon by the user, that the vendor is not interested in enforcement (waiver). To avoid

that problem, it is wise for vendors to periodically enforce audit rights, even if only by a letter of inquiry. Otherwise, what is lost may never be regained--and that could jeopardize the vendor's ability to assure "secrecy" of its proprietary product.

How long does a trade secret last? The technical answer, assuming all things being equal, is forever. But realistically, products rapidly lose their competitive edge. Enforcement of restrictions for a non-competitive product is a meaningless exercise. So, if a vendor finds that its "secret" product is not that secret, the vendor should focus resources on maintaining the secrecy of those proprietary products that are still competitive. In essence, enforcement should be consistent but selective.

The Fine Line: An important question facing every software vendor and employee is what information can be legitimately "taken" by the employee on termination. As discussed, material identified by the employer as a trade secret, providing the employer has acted to publicize and protect its "secret" nature, cannot be taken. But does that include skills, methodologies or ideas learned on the job? Take the example of a high tech organization that was working on miniaturization of electronic components. One of its employees, an engineer, became interested in drawing "electronic circuit masks" on silicon chips. While on the employer's time and using its facilities, the engineer began experimenting with new technology to accomplish that objective. Discussions with the employer brought a lack of interest in pursuing that technology. Subsequently, the employee left and formed his own organization, which eventually supplied to the former employer, silicon chips bearing electronic circuit masks. Even though the technology was developed while using the former employer's resources, its clear lack of interest in that technology gave that ex-employee a free hand. This "safe harbor" (lack of employer interest) was enhanced by the non-competitive relationship between the employer and its former employee was marketing a technology that did not compete for the employer's market. Conclusion: technology developed while working for an employer, using its facilities and time, can be "taken" by the employee on termination, if it is non-competitive and if the employer has expressed disinterest.

Now another step. Suppose the employee develops technology desired by the employer during the course of employment. Further, suppose the employee quits, takes only his personal notes, and goes to work for a competitor. While working for that competitor, the employee uses the lessons learned in his previous environment to help the competitor create a product that threatens the previous employer's market. Has the employee exposed himself, and his new employer to a charge of "piracy" and unfair competition? The answer is unequivocally yes! The key is that the employee took his personal notes, developed while working for his former employer. Those notes belonged to that employer, and their use for a competitor's benefit was a violation of confidentiality. The lesson: an employee should take no personal notes, or documents of any kind developed while working for an employer. Unlike the first example, the terminating employee threatened his former employer's market with competitive technology initially developed on that employer's time and at its expense.

* An employee can take technology developed while working for his employer if that technology is non-competitive and if the employer has expressed no interest in it. In such a circumstance there is no theft of trade secrets.

* An employee cannot take technology developed while working for an employer if that

employer has expressed a proprietary (ownership) interest, and particularly if that technology creates or maintains a market for that employer.

There is a gray area between those two poles. For example, a bank developed a software product necessary to track and control all electronic funds transfers. A key person in the development of that product was a programmer. She subsequently left the bank, taking no proprietary information of any kind, not even personal notes. Working for a competitor, she helped it develop a substantially similar product. Did she violate any duty of confidentiality to her former employer because she used "lessons learned" to help a competitor enhance its market position? The answer would be "no." Unlike the second example, she took only the mental techniques and abilities learned while working for her employer. Ideas and experience cannot be locked up. Since no notes or documents were taken, her former employer would have little basis for claiming theft of trade secrets.

Allegations of theft are often difficult for an employee to defend. Everyone usually takes some notes, diagrams or materials home during the course of employment. This makes it almost impossible for the employee to prove that work for a competitor was based solely on mentally retained techniques or experience. Making matters worse, employers often use "theft" allegations as excuses to stifle legitimate competition. To avoid the trauma of defending against spurious trade secret theft allegations, the employee should:

* Give the employer reasonable advance notice of his departure--thereby permitting a slow phase-out from key projects--and, to avoid surprise, make sure the employer knows that his new job will involve a competitor.

* Give up all loose ends so that the employer cannot claim sabotage (don't burn bridges), and cooperate as much as possible so that termination is a friendly rather than a stressful event.

* Take no documents or material belonging to the employers. (This includes any notes personally developed by the employee during the course of employment.)

In essence, be friendly, reasonable and honest. A case in point is Bridge Technology, where IBM used its muscle to squash a new company created by former employees, who did everything wrong! While working on a project related to development of the IBM Personal Computer (P.C.) three engineers formed a separate company called Bridge Technology. They then offered a competitor IBM-developed technology related to the P.C. Remarkably, the competitor proved honest, reporting the matter to IBM which:

* fired the three engineers;

* sued them and their new company for wages paid after the new company was formed; and

* sought an injunction against use of any of the information acquired while working for IBM.

Although the case was settled out of court, IBM won all three major points. Lesson: don't start a new organization until employment has been terminated, don't contact any customer (or competitive) prospects while employed, and don't take any material deemed proprietary by the employer.

IBM's example of using litigation against former employees has been followed by numerous high tech companies, often resulting in allegations that litigation has been used as a tool to stifle competition. Whether such allegations are true or not, the employee can discourage such action by playing it straight. Don't take anything, don't contact any prospects, and don't create (or work) for a rival organization prior to terminating employment.

Employee Innovation: The line between what is claimed as proprietary by the employer and what is an original invention by the employee can be murky.

Take the DP engineer who was hired to do programming for a CAD/CAM manufacturer. This person had no express contract with his employer assigning all interests in inventions developed during the course of employment. While working for that employer, the engineer, during coffee- and lunch-breaks, developed a software spreadsheet product for micro computers. Since the product was limited in function, the market would be home (non-business) use. The DP engineer sold all marketing rights to a software distributing company. The employer learned of the product and how it was developed, and demanded all royalties. Was that employer entitled to royalties derived from the sale of a software product developed on "company time"? Answering that question requires a response to several preliminary questions:

175

* Was the employee hired to invent? Although there was no specific contract dictating the purpose of employment, it was clear that the employee was hired to create or modify software program codes; in essence, to solve software coding problems so that applications pertinent to business needs could be developed or maintained. Implied in all that rhetoric is the assumption that sometime during the course of employment the employee might "invent" something in order to solve a problem related to the employer's business requirements. So the answer is an implied "yes"--a DP engineer is impliedly hired to invent.

* If the engineer was hired to invent, did the inventor use his employer's time and facilities to create the software product? Even though the employee did most of the work on "break time" provided by the employer, there is no question that the latter's resources were used to create that product. Thinking, planning and creating took place during work hours (coffee- and lunch-breaks). Computer facilities, owned by the employer, were used to develop the software invention. Even stationary, bearing the employer's logo, was used to contact the software distributer and consummate the contract. So the answer is an unequivocal yes, the invention was developed on the

employer's time and with its resources.

* Was the invention related to the employer's trade or business? If the answer is "yes," all questions stop--because the employer owns the product. However, in this case, the employer's prime market was the manufacture of CAD/CAM hardware and software for other manufacturing companies. Spreadsheet analysis software, designed for personal computers had no relationship whatsoever to the employer's trade or business. So the answer is "no," because the software product is unrelated to the employer's trade or business and ownership is therefore vested in the employee.

* Does the employer then have any rights to an invention that was created by an employee during working hours, where that product was unrelated to the employer's business? The answer is "yes," fairness dictates that the employer should have a free right of use, called "shopright." This right, however, is personal, meaning it cannot be sold or assigned.

Based on these questions and answers it is clear that:

1)   The employee must be hired either directly by agreement, or impliedly through the type of work performed, to invent.

2)   The employee must use the employer's resources to develop the invention.   There are questions about how much is enough (use of resources) to give the employer a proprietary right.   Answering them is like asking how many angels can dance on the head of a pin. Suffice it to say that any degree of resource involvement, even if minimal, is enough to give an employer the right to claim an interest.

3)   The employee's invention must be related to the employer's trade or business. If there is any relationship, no matter how slight, the employer has a strong claim of interest. Of course, if there is no relationship, then the employer owns a shopright (personal right of usage).

Clearly, if the employee wants to invent and to

"own" that invention, then development should be on the employee's time and he should use his own resources.

IBM's policy on protecting innovation while respecting employee rights is clearly described by Frank T. Cary, IBM's Board Chairman, in an interview with the Harvard Business Review reprinted here, with permission, in its entirety.

IBM'S GUIDELINES TO EMPLOYEE PRIVACY
An interview with Frank T. Cary

Probably no organization in the world has taken the stance that IBM has on the question of employee privacy. The company has gone far beyond any legal requirements and the recommendations of most writers and legislators in protecting employees at all levels from the collection of unnecessary personal information and from improper use of personal data in the files. A remarkable aspect of this story is that management established its policy not in response to any demands of activists or others but on its own initiative, out of a conviction that such steps are right. With the privacy issue on the minds of legislators, civil liberties authorities, and many other Americans, IBM's approach should be practical interest to many business leaders. In this interview, Frank T. Cary describes the principal guidelines at IBM and their implementation.

Mr. Cary is chairman of the board and chief executive officer of IBM. He joined the company in 1948, became an assistant branch manager in San Francisco in 1954, and was named manager of the Chicago downtown office in 1956. He held a number of divisional and corporate posts before becoming president of the Data Processing Division in 1964. He was named senior vice president in 1967 and elected to the board in 1968. In 1971 he was elected president of IBM, and in 1973 he became chairman and chief executive officer. He is a director or a trustee of several well-known organizations.

The interview with Mr. Cary was conducted by David W. Ewing, HBR's executive editor-planning, and Wanda A. Lankenner, editorial assistant.

Digitized imaging courtesy of Computer Sketch, Inc.

Photographs by Derrick Te Paske.

HBR: Mr. Cary, you and other members of IBM's top management have spent a great deal of time working out an original approach to employee privacy. Why does this problem concern you so much?

Cary: Organizations have invaded people's privacy with

steel file cabinets and manila folders for years. But computer systems with remote access have intensified both the problem and public concern. When I became chairman, it seemed to me that this subject was going to become an issue for us, as auto safety has become a major issue for Ford and General Motors. In years past we tended to step back, in the belief that others should take the lead-professors, politicians, lawyers. Now we have got to take some leadership and try to think our way through the subject. Privacy is not a passing fad.

Are the policies adopted by IBM applicable to business and government organizations in general?

Some of the things we've done are feasible in other organizations, but we have long recognized that we cannot solve many issues of individual privacy before the country solves them. We have to keep our efforts in the context of our business--we don't have any special competence to tell the world how legislators and privacy commissions and other groups should resolve all the questions being debated.

What part of the privacy issue, then, is of most concern to IBM?

Personal information about employees--the material that management keeps in files and data banks. This is a big part of the privacy issue but certainly not all of it. For instance, some hotly debated questions have to do with protection against intrusion by government agencies and the collection of census data. We don't have special competence in matters like those.

Have IBM employees influenced your concern with privacy?

Thomas Watson, Sr. and Jr. both had very strong beliefs in the dignity of the individual, but privacy in particular didn't begin to get special attention until the middle 1960s. That was when an IBM employee asked one day to see his personal folder. The question ended up in the office of Thomas J. Watson, Jr. After he reviewed it thoroughly, his answer to the employee was yes. He then wrote to all IBM managers, saying that employees throughout the company ought to be able to see their personal folders. The subject has been growing with us ever since.

After becoming chief executive in 1973, you began giving privacy a higher priority than it had received in the past. How did you decide you had a problem?

When we looked at employee privacy in IBM from the top down, things appeared to be pretty good. We seemed to be handling personal data in a sensitive and careful way. But then we organized a corporate task force to look at the subject from the bottom up. At different IBM sites, local task forces were organized to find out what actually was being done. We found that in some cases information about employees was being handled in a way that we didn't like, that seemed to violate our principles.

What sort of things?

Oh, information in managers' informal files that shouldn't have been there, such as a piece of hearsay. Uses of information that shouldn't have been allowed, such as when an outsider requested more than routine facts about an employee.

Then how did you go about changing these practices?

I assigned some of our very best people to work on the problem. Also, I brought in Professor Alan Westin of Columbia, an authority on civil liberities, to serve as a consultant. After much creative thought and analysis, they would bring their ideas and proposals to me, and then I'd do what I like to call "put English on the ball." That is, I would give the recommendations some thought of my own and add my personal support in implementation--meetings with key management people, speeches, letters, and editorials in <u>Think</u>, our employee publication.

Was there much employee reaction to your efforts?

The changes we made weren't being demanded by employees and didn't come as any great surprise to them, because in the past we had been paying attention to some of these needs. But I think that what we've done generally is considered by employees to be a good thing. Of course, we don't have all the answers even today. Our approach and thinking keep evolving.

What kind of feedback do you get from employees?

We do get some feedback on privacy questions through our "Speak Up!" program. "Speak Up!" is a system of communicating problems and questions to higher levels of management when they're not handled to an employee's satisfaction by his or her manager. The employee remains anonymous--no one knows the employee's name except the coordinator in the "Speak-Up!" office.

"Speak Up!" complaints about privacy have been minimal, but they indicate a widespread awareness of the issue. After you decide on privacy guidelines, how do you make sure they're followed?

We try to make it very, very clear to managers what's expected of them. The rules for handling personal information are incorporated in our management training programs. We describe the principles we want followed, and we walk them through the specific do's and don'ts of practicing the rules. We try to produce uniform understanding on this. Within 30 days of becoming a manager, every first-line manager begins to receive basic training.

In addition, we ask all IBMers to help by bringing to management's attention infringements of personal privacy in their areas of the business. And we ask every employee to refrain from any practice that would unnecessarily invade the privacy of others.

What happens to a manager or other employee who violates a guideline?

Depending on the violation, the manager may be subject to dismissal. It's very clear-cut what we're trying to do, and I think everyone understands that we mean it. If there's confusion for some legitimate reason--and there may be, because it's hard to anticipate all situations--we make allowances for error. But there have been cases when the manager has gotten into trouble.

It is fair to say that people are penalized more severely for infractions of ethical standards at IBM than for, say, lapses in performance?

I think that failures in ethics and integrity here are less excusable than errors in performance. People can perform their jobs on a range from satisfactory to outstanding, but there's only one standard of ethics and integrity that we recognize. So, yes, there are two levels of assessment.

What kinds of problems has IBM had in developing general understanding of your privacy guidelines?

We've had little difficulty communicating the procedures. What information it is permissible to ask a job applicant for, what information goes where, who can use it, what is available to line managers versus what is available only to medical people--all of that has been formalized, and there's been little confusion about it. Where there's been a problem is in what the privacy rules mean for the manager-employee relationship. There was a tendency for some managers to think that privacy meant a change in the way they should be involved with their people.

What mistakes were your managers making?

They were withdrawing. This really worried me. We've always encouraged managers to have strong relationships with employees and to be interested and helpful to them. Partly because of the term privacy, I think, some managers began retreating from involvement. That wasn't what we wanted them to do.

Could you give us an example of managerial withdrawal?

I'll have to make it a hypothetical case. Suppose one of our managers got an anonymous letter giving strong indication that an employee was a child beater. The manager might judge this to be a private matter and not investigate. Of course he would be wrong. Humanitarian considerations aside, an accusation such as this, if true, might affect both the employee's performance and-- if there were contact with customers--ability to represent IBM. The manager should not leave the problem unattended. He would have to investigate the situation. The manager should not interpret privacy to mean "Let people alone"?

That's right. To give you a real, rather extreme example, a group of employees who listened to what we were saying about privacy mistakenly applied the idea to office design. They said we weren't respecting the privacy of employees because we weren't letting them have private offices. Finally, we realized what was happening. Some employees were reading into the word privacy their concerns for physical privacy. So we decided to be more precise by using the term personal information.

IBM employs some 130,000 people in countries overseas. Are they subject to the same guidelines as people in the United States?

The rules aren't applied formally in all other countries, because of differing customs and traditions. For instance, it wouldn't make sense to apply the same rules to IBMers in Japan. But the basic principles of our approach have been adopted in other countries like these, or are under review there, and I think these principles will be in practice in all countries before long.

Let's turn now to the specific everyday rules that IBM follows--the practices and policies that make this subject real from the standpoint of employees. We would like to start at the beginning, when information on an employee first accumulates. What personal information do you ask for on a job application?

Only what we think is necessary to make the employment decision--name, address, previous employer, education, and a few other basic facts. We don't even ask for date of birth at this time, although if the person is hired we will need to get his or her age. We don't ask about the employment of the applicant's spouse, about relatives employed by IBM, or for previous addresses. We don't ask about any prior treatment for nervous disorder or mental illness. We don't ask about arrest records or pending criminal charges or criminal indictments. We do ask about convictions--but only convictions during the previous five years.

IBM used to ask for some of the information now omitted. What made you change your mind?

We were getting a lot of data we really didn't need. It
was cluttering up the files. Worse than that, it was
tagging along after people. Particularly in the case of
unfavorable information about an employee, there's a
tendency for the material to follow the person around
forever and to influence management decisions that it
shouldn't. It's better not to have the data in the
files in the first place.

But can you be sure in advance what personal information
is going to be relevant?

No. But you know what you need at the time, for just
this decision. Later you can collect more data as
needed. This is part of the problem, you see. There's
a common attitude that "It doesn't hurt to have all this
information, it can't do any harm, so why not get it?"
That's what we're working against. When we looked into
this problem a few years ago, we found that it could
indeed do harm to have information that wasn't of
current relevance. For example, information about how
young or how old a person is, or about an arrest a
couple of years ago--it shouldn't influence the hiring
decision, but it might do so if it were on hand. So we
decided the best thing to do was simply not to collect
it.

What about appraisals of the applicant's strengths and weaknesses--do you cut back on that information, too?

Not at all. Just the opposite. Good interviewing becomes the key. Our people are very good at this, and we count on them to draw applicants out and understand their interests.

What about verifying the statements an applicant makes?

We used to employ outside credit agencies to do background checking on prospective employees, but not any more. When we feel that a reference on education or previous employment should be checked, our own people do it. Incidentally, they do it with the knowledge and consent of the applicant.

Inevitably there are some things we don't catch, but I don't think they are material enough to make it worthwhile to go through all the routines we used to have to go through. When we used to do background checks on applicants, for example, the information gathered would sometimes include data that just wasn't germane.

We're interested in employment testing. Some critics

feel that tests can be an invasion of privacy. What's IBM's stance here?

We have stopped excursions into applicants' emotional and private lives through the use of personality tests. We don't use polygraphs in hiring or at any other time-- we never have. But we use aptitude tests and consider them useful. Some tests have credibility, for instance, in forecasting a person's aptitude for programming, or typing, or certain other types of occupation. Also, this sort of information isn't so personal or sensitive. It's more job-related than personality tests are.

What about tests of an applicant's general intelligence?

They don't help us much, either. Many of the people we hire have college backgrounds, and their records in college seem to be as good an indicator as any I.Q. test. So here again, since there are other ways of making the evaluation we need--ways that can't be intrusions--we use them instead.

This brings us to the next stage. Do you try to control the buildup of personal information on an employee after he or she is hired?

Yes, we work pretty hard on that. We keep purging data that no longer seems relevant. Performance appraisals usually are kept for three years only--in unusual cases, for five years. All grades and appraisals from IBM course instructors are kept for three years only. A record of a conviction is thrown out after three years. Then there's all that information many managers keep on an employee's attendance, performance, vacation schedules, and so on. We tell managers to keep this material for a limited time only.

How much of the onus is on operating managers, rather than on the personnel department, to keep the files stripped down to essentials?

Since there are some files operating managers never examine, obviously the personnel department has to purge them of old data. But we hold individual managers responsible for seeing that job-related information, which they do see, is kept to a minimum. Now, the personnel department is responsible for developing guidelines, and it may check up on the manager to see that the purging is done, but he or she can't pass the buck. We say, in effect, "This is your job, and you know what the rules are--they're not terribly complex. It is up to you to see that the rules are followed."

Let's talk now about who can look at an employee's files. First, what can IBM line managers see?

Any job-related information they are allowed to see. The distinction between job-related and non-job-related is important to the privacy question. An employee's performance appraisals, performance plans, letters of commendation, records of awards, sales records, production assignments, and so on--all such job-related information is kept available for the line manager to see. The manager needs to see it to make decisions. The only other people who can inspect this material are those with a need to know, such as a manager considering the employee for a new position.

Is there anything the line manager can't see?

Yes. Every large company has to have quite a bit of personal information on an employee that has little or nothing to do with work performance. So this information is out of bounds for the line manager. This file is open only to the personnel and financial departments. It includes medical benefits data, records of personal finances such as wage garnishments, payroll deductions, life insurance beneficiaries, payments for educational programs, house valuations, and so on.

These items are required to administer benefit plans, to meet the company's legal obligations, and to carry out other aspects of personnel administration, but the operating manager does not need to know them.

By this division, we protect the individual from having facts about his or her life accessible to people who should only be concerned with specific areas.

Numerous employees, attorneys, and civil liberties leaders are incensed because much personal information in the files of many employers may be released to outsiders--often without the employee's knowledge. How does IBM handle that issue?

If an outsider wants to verify that a person works for us, we will release the most recent job title the person has, the most recent place of work, and the date of employment at IBM. We'll do this much without contacting the employee. But if the outsider wants to know the person's salary, or wants a five-year job chronology, we don't give out that information without written approval from the employee.

As for creditors, attorneys, private agencies, and others desiring non-job-related information, we give out none of it without the employee's consent, unless the law requires disclosure by us.

We honor legitimate requests for information from government agencies, though we require the investigators to furnish proper identification, prove their legal authority, and demonstrate that they need the information sought. If a district attorney's office is making a criminal investigation, we cooperate within limits. It's hard to make rules to cover all situations that may arise, but we have specialists in the legal and personnel departments who use their judgment in an unusual situation, and they handle these problems pretty well.

Do you protect IBM's 600,000 or so stockholders in the same way?

Yes. Not long ago, for example, a U.S. senator wrote us asking for the names and holdings of IBM's 30 top stockholders. He had no subpoena. He would give no purpose for his inquiry, even after we asked. So we refused to give him the data he wanted. Suppose he had spelled out his purpose. Then, I suppose, we might have taken the next step and asked the permission of the 30 stockholders involved to release the facts.

Social security numbers have been a sore spot with people concerned about privacy. How does IBM deal with this problem?

Some organizations seem to think so, but we won't put social security numbers on company badges or identification cards. Also, we have taken them off all IBM medical cards; insurance companies get an IBM employee identification number when they process a medical or dental claim.

We've discussed access to an employee's files by operating managers, the personnel department, and outsiders. What, if anything, can the employee himself or herself see?

With just a few exceptions, employees can see what's in their personnel folders--job-related information as well as non-job-related. We want them to know what's there-- no suprises. If they find something to quarrel with, they can ask for a correction. The key document, of course, is the performance appraisal. But there's less curiosity about this than you would think, and the reason is that the manager has already told the employee how he or she was rated. That was done when the appraisal session was held. In fact, the manager's appraisal that contains the ratings is reviewed by the employee, at which time he or she can add comments.

What are the exceptions--what data cannot be seen?

Employees can't see notes on "Open Door" investigations of complaints they made. At IBM, the "Open Door" is a system for allowing employees to take a grievance over their supervisors' heads to a higher management level. The employee identifies himself or herself (in this respect, the "Open Door" system is different from "Speak Up!"), so the case goes into a special file, which, by the way, has very stringent access and retention standards. As chief executive, I'm the court of last resort, so to speak, and many cases come to me. I assign an executive to investigate each situation, and I personally review the findings.   During the investigations, these senior managers talk to many people and get honest, frank answers to many tough questions. They couln't get such candid answers if they didn't talk off the record, in strict confidence. So we don't allow an employee to see the notes made on a case he or she was concerned with. If we did, the "Open Door" system wouldn't work.

Can the employee learn anything at all about the investigation?

Oh, yes. The investigator sits down with the employee after the inquiries are completed and reports the conclusion. Some of the specific findings may be discussed. But the investigator doesn't quote the people interviewed, and doesn't show the file to the employee concerned.

Do some of your assistants specialize in "Open Door" cases?

No one spends full time on them. We select different people on the basis of position occupied, objectivity, reputation for fairness, and so on. Also, we never ask the manager who has been criticized to do the investigation. We have strict ground rules for this, and I do have assistants who spend considerable time overviewing the system and seeing that the rules are followed. That the investigators start out taking the side of the complainants is an important rule. Quite often, they end up on that side--they find that the complainant is right.

Can an employee see information about salary plans for himself or herself?

Our managers make salary forecasts for their employees as a matter of course in business planning. In effect, a manager says, "I expect to increase so-and-so's salary by this much on such-and-such a date." We don't consider this personal information. It's business planning information and subject to change. Once the increase is acted on, the data become personal information, but until then the figures are not available to the employee concerned.

In fact, such figures are not kept in the employee's file but in some place like the desk drawer of the manager.

Is information about an employee's promotion prospects handled in the same way?

Yes. Again, it's just good planning technique to know who is ready to take over the management jobs at certain levels. We prepare replacement tables with the names of, say, the top three candidates for every one of those jobs. Now, there are surely people who would love to see those tables and know who will be moved up if a certain individual gets hit by a streetcar the next day. But this, too, is business planning, not personal information, and so it's not available for employees to see. Besides, it would be misleading and misunderstood. We do not always do what is written in the replacement planning tables. Nor do we always give the amount of salary increase that is forcast.

Another thing many civil liberties spokesmen and others are unhappy about is the practice of recording employee conversations without the person's consent. What is IBM policy here?

There's absolutely no taping of a person's conversations on the telephone without express permission, or at business meetings without prior announcement. I consider this a simple matter of respect for the individual.

Were conversations ever recorded in the past?

Yes, I think it was done sometimes. Some time ago, an employee had a hidden tape recorder he used for recording some sales calls he made on customers. He did it innocently, I think--for his own use to analyze what transpired. I think you just do not record conversations with customers or prospects or anyone else without telling them first. People act differently depending on the kind of talk they think they're having--recorded or not recorded, on the record or off, for a newspaper or for TV. As the saying goes, the medium is the message. I think it's the same principle that has influenced the courts to keep television out of the courtroom.

What about an employee's off-the-job behavior? Many Americans apparently feel that employers want to know too much about what an employee does after hours.

We're careful about that, too. In 1968 Thomas Watson, Jr., then chairman, wrote a letter to managers stating that management was concerned with off-the-job behavior only when it impaired a person's ability to perform regular job assignments--their own or others'--or when it affected the reputation of the company in a major way. That statement has continued to be our guideline.

Yet IBM has a reputation for being solicitous about employee welfare, as you pointed out earlier. Isn't it hard to draw the line?

Yes, because when a manager is trying to be helpful and when he's getting "nosey" is something that different people see in different ways. So you have to use judgment here. You can't have hard and fast rules. Certainly, spying of any kind is out. But what about a manager who visits an employee who is sick in the hospital or at home? Such a visit can be considered an invasion of privacy, given certain circumstances. So the manager has to be sensitive to the person and situation in order to do the right thing.

In _Think_, IBM's publication for employees, an interesting problem was posed: An engineer goes on vacation and forgetfully leaves some confidential new product specificatons in his desk drawer. Is his privacy being invaded if his manager goes into the drawer to get the specifications when needed?

In one sense, there's no violation, because desks and files are IBM property. But the manager must have a very good reason for looking. No one should be fooling around in someone else's papers. Of course, it's important to try to avoid this sort of situation. When a person leaves on vacation or a trip, he or she should leave any business documents that might be needed in the hands of someone else who will carry on.

One hotly debated topic is management control of an employee's involvement with outside organizations. Could you comment on this question?

We ask employees who want to become involved in public problems and want to take a position on them to do so as private individuals, not on behalf of IBM. They should make that clear to the press. But only if there is a potential conflict of interest do we ask employees to excuse themselves from the discussion and any decision or to vote on it. This might be the case if, say, the employee sat on a board of education and the board were going to vote on an IBM proposal. (1)

(Copyright 1976, Harvard Business Review).

(5) <u>Overview</u>

<u>Trade Secret</u>: The proprietary device called a trade secret is powerful. It protects both the idea and the manner in which it is manifested. But it is also fragile--subject to loss through unauthorized disclosure, reverse engineering, innocent access or independent discovery. Protecting the trade secret has given rise to a profusion of contracts and covenants, as well as of internal security requirements, all designed to discourage unauthorized distribution. Is there a better way of protecting

innovation, preserving the competitive edge while permitting aggressive marketing?

C.   Copyright

A copyright protects the form in which an idea is expressed. Suppose a software product expresses an idea but only as it is used in that code (form of expression). If a competitor seizes upon that same idea and expresses it by using a totally different form of code, then the first copyright has not been infringed.

Unlike a trade secret, copyright does not protect the idea, but only the form of expression. Why then has copyright become such an important tool in preserving proprietary interests in new technology? Because, it is based on federal statutory law and provides for specific damages if an infringement occurs. In addition, a registered copyright is easier to prove, because all that is needed is the formal certificate of registration. With a trade secret, the owner must first prove using evidentiary procedures, that the product meets all the legal requirements of a trade secret. Finally, a copyright is not terminated by disclosure, whether authorized or otherwise. Reverse engineering, independent discovery, or innocent access have no effect on the owner's proprietary interest established by statute. Once filed (first in time is first in right), the copyright continues for 50 years plus the author's life.

(1)   Existence and Filing: A copyright exists when ink touches paper, or is fixed in a magnetic media such as a floppy disk--either being the moment the idea is expressed. No strange forms or rituals are needed (unlike a trade secret) to secure a copyright.   Why then filing?   Because in this bad world of thieves, pirates, and others who prey on creative minds, proof of ownership (proprietary interest), like in the old west, is much simpler if there is an authorized registration (like a deed) from the U.S. Copyright Office.   Once that registration is in hand, opponents have the difficult burden of proving that the form of expression was not "copyrightable" or that they had it first.

Registration is simplicity itself:

* Telephone the U.S. Copyright Office hotline for forms. The current number is (202) 287-9100.   Ask for the "TX" and be prepared to wait approximately one week.

* Filling out the form requires little in the way of legal or technical education.   Just follow instructions.   If there is a question call (202) 287-8700.   Unfortunately, since this number is usually busy it is wise to work out the solution yourself.

206

* Place a copyright notice on each of the software programs. The notice should be placed in a prominent location, such as below the program's name.

* The form of notice consists of the word "Copyright," followed by the year of first publication (when the program was first registered or used) and the owner's name. An example of a sufficient copyright notice is "Copyright, 1984, Bruce K. Brickman, Esq."

* In addition, it doesn't hurt to add, below the copyright notice, "All rights reserved, any use or publication without the owner's permission is strictly prohibited." This language, although legally gratuitous (not necessary to preserve the copyright), is sufficent to deter the uninitiated, by explaining the nature of the copyright notice

* Complete and forward the form, along with ten (10) dollars and one copy of the source code printout, including the title page containing the copyright notice, to the Copyright Office (address is provided on the form). If the program exceeds 50 pages then include only the first 25 and last 25 pages, the middle portion is deemed registered. If there are a series of programs (such as a system) which create an integrated and compatible product, then send in

the first 25 pages of a program (arbitrarily nominated as the first program) the first ten pages of each successive program, except for the final program, where the last 25 pages are included.

Processing copyright applications takes approximately 16 weeks. Thereafter, an authorized registration is returned.

What type of software programs can be copyrighted? Virtually any software program, regardless of similarity to others, can be copyrighted. However, to be "copyrightable" the software program cannot be in the public domain. This means that it cannot be a product, such as Basic, Cobol or Fortran, generally known to be used by software vendors or customers. In essence, the software product must be original, and the author must have contributed "creativity" in the course of its formulation. Originality often means "unique," such as combining known concepts into a new pattern to create a product that did not exist previously.

Illustrative of "original" are the software programs designed for word processing. There are many such application programs on the market, but none is exactly like another. Each has a creative twist or feature differentiating it from others. In effect, although the same idea is involved, the manner of expression is uniquely different for each word processing software product. A copyright fails if there is evidence that the difference is trivial, such as a minor change in coding. In one case, the court noted that the programmer bodily lifted the coding structure and syntax from a copyrighted product, making only minor changes that had no affect on the overall coding logic. For that reason, the court found an infringement. The author must be prepared to prove that the software program was creatively formulated and is not a "generous copy" of another person's product.

The beauty of registration is that non-infringement is presumed until proved by the party contesting the copyright. This burden of disproving a valid copyright is expensive and difficult, and discouraging to most who try. In the <u>Apple vs. Franklin</u> case, one of the arguments rejected by the appellate court was that the operating code contained on a chip (Read Only Memory) was not "copyrightable" because it was part of the machine, and therefore, not a written expression of an idea. This argument was rejected, partly because of the presumption of "copyrightability" derived from registration.

Another advantage of copyright registration is the right to bring an action for infringement. To get into court, the copyright must be registered. Upon proving infringement, the winner is entitled to statutory damages ($10,000)--not a hefty sum, but the purpose of copyright is to stop or prevent rather than to collect.

Finally, registration gives the damaged party a right to claim atorneys fees--a right seldom granted in civil litigation. Altogether, the presumption of "copyrightability," treble damages and attorneys fees provide a potent form of proprietary protection for the expression of ideas, but not for the underlying idea itself.

2. <u>Application</u>: Let us now apply that introduction to the nature and effect of copyright to some practical circumstances. Assume that the source code for a software product has been copyrighted; then ask:

* Does the same copyright protect the object code? The answer is Yes! Under the new (1980) modifications to the 1976 Copyright Act, adaptations of the copyrighted source are protected by the original copyright.

* Does this extended umbrella of protection, based on adaptations, encompass more than the object code?

There is a gray area as to what is included within the term "adaptation." For example, modifications would be included if the original source code had not been substantially changed. This means that the underlying logic structure of the code remains essentially the same, with the modifications focusing on adjustments rather than wholesale alterations in the program. But what about an enhancement to the software product where a new feature is added to the program's performance application? This often causes much gnashing of teeth over how "substantial" the alteration is. Probably the safest course is to register the enhanced product to avoid a challenge that the newly enhanced software program exceeds the criteria for "adaptation."

Certainly fixes curing effort would be within that criteria, as would documentation such as flow chart, user manual and other written material describing the product and its features. It is important that all written material contain the copyright notice, to avoid an "honest" misunderstanding.

* If the object code is contained on a silicon chip does that chip have to physically contain a copyright notice imprinted on its surface?

There was some judicial thinking to that effect, but fortunately good sense prevailed and the courts now require that the program recite a copyright notice. This was also a key issue in the <u>Apple</u> <u>vs</u> <u>Franklin</u> case, which was resolved in Apple's favor. To have found otherwise would have impeded technological advancement, since a silicon chip has little room for a copyright notice in addition to the electronic circuitry diagrammed on its surface.

* Can copyright and trade secret protection coexist?

Theoretically, the answer should be no, but that is not the case. The key is "limited" distribution. Suppose, for example, a software program contains both a notice of copyright and trade secret protection. The software vendor has distributed the product through license agreements to end-users. This means that only those authorized by written license are permitted to use that product. A competitor working as a consultant to a licensed end-user accesses the software product's user-manual and, through reverse engineering, determines the logic for that product's source code. The competitor then creates a product with substantially distinct modifications in its logic. Has that competitor misappropriated the original vendor's secret or infringed on its copyright?

To answer that question a court noted the following facts:

* The software product was limited to distribution by license;

* The copyright notice does not automatically mean public dissemination of the product, but merely registration in the Copyright Office;

* The rival competitor knew that the document it accessed would describe a trade secret owned by another software vendor;

* The licensed user knew it breached a confidential relationship with the licensing vendor for that product, by showing the user manual to the competitor.

Based on those facts the court concluded that the software product's trade secret nature was not automatically preempted by a copyright notice. Only if the product was distributed to the general public on a non-exclusive basis would the trade secret become ineffective. Since distribution was by license then it was limited, and the product's trade secret nature was not compromised. The fact that a copyright notice existed would have no automatic affect on the viability of the trade secret.

With that conclusion settled, the court issued an

injunction against the rival for so long as it would take that entity to pay the product's development costs. The result: both the underlying idea and the manner of expression were protected.

3. Changes in Concept: Coexistance of trade secret and copyright in the same product is a relatively new idea. It evolved as a consequence of the new technology, and all courts might not feel comfortable with the doctrine. Even if this concept is generally accepted, the definition of limited distribution will still not be settled. For instance, a popular software product, such as Wordstar, has been distributed to hundreds of thousands of users. The method of distribution is by a license which recites that product's trade secret nature as well as the copyright notice. Does it seem reasonable that trade secret protection should exist for a product so widely distributed? If the answer is yes, the effect of dual protection on such a wide scale could chill evolution of new technology, since many inventors borrow ideas from existing products. As the saying goes, "there's nothing new under the sun!" If those inventors were suddenly confronted with a misappropriation and infringement charges for using widely distributed ideas, the growth of new technology would be impaired. So the line on coexistance of trade secret and copyright is not yet firm.

Another change in concept has been the expansion of copyright. A leading video game manufacturer copyrighted the arcade screen display as well as the source code for its popular game. A rival produced a video game with a similar, but not identical, screen operated by different source code programming. The leading manufacturer sued its rival for infringement of copyright. The court noted that the rival's video game portrayed ideas similar to those in the manufacturer's copyrighted game. It granted that there was different software, and even differences in the displays, but main characters were similar and the games had the same objectives. For those reasons, the court found that the "underlying ideas" were the same, and granted the injunction. As a result, copyright has been expanded to protect the manner of expression and the underlying idea. Again, such an expansion would eliminate the need for trade secret. More importantly, it would "chill" creativity, since virtually all similar applications share the same "underlying ideas", thereby excluding them from the creative pool.

Fortunately, other courts have not yet followed that decision. It is still safe to argue that in most instances trade secret protects the limited distribution of an idea and its manner of expression, while copyright protects the mass distribution of how an idea is expressed.

The effect of unsettled law on users of innovation is to add a degree of anxiety to the transaction. The old definitions of copyright and trade secret are no longer reliable. During this period, while courts try to grapple with innovation and to fit the technology into existing proprietary devices, decisions will be inconsistent (if not sometimes incoherent). For that reason, caution is the watchword. Users should rely on well drawn, understandable documents that mean what they say and that conform to established proprietary devices.

(4). The Significance of Apple vs. Franklin: Protection for new technology. The present copyright law protects the registered source code and its adaptations. Apple embedded the object code for application software programs on chips. The court held that even though embedded on silicon chips, the object code was protected as an adaptation of the source code. Further--and even more important--Apple's operating code for its computers was also embedded on silicon chips. Franklin argued that the operating software was not decipherable, except by another machine, and therefore could not be considered an "expression" of ideas within the Copyright Act. In essence, if a person cannot read the program printout, it is not "copyrightable." The appellate court disagreed with Franklin's argument. It held that the Copyright Act permits the use of a machine to "express" ideas. In other words, the operating code is "copyrightable" even if it is intelligible only to another machine.

Why is this case significant? Dollars! Silicon chips are the key to the high tech industries' current thrust to shrink product size while increasing power. New machines will, like Apple's computers, have the operating and application programs embedded in silicon chips. If manufacturers cannot protect their proprietary interest, then advances in technology would be jeopardized and costs might not fall so rapidly as would otherwise be the case. Both developments would be detrimental to the consumer. The Apple vs Franklin decision will speed the migration from diskettes to chips, permitting innovators to benefit from their creativity.

(5). Copyright Overview: Clearly, times are changing! The old definition of "copyrightable" concepts focusing on the manner in which an idea is expressed is being stretched to encompass the evolution of new technology. Copyright and trade secret are being brought closer together, raising the alternate danger of too much protection "chilling" innovation. Chip masks, containing software code, are apparently not yet protected by the expanded Copyright Act, spurring an intensive lobbying effort in Congress. But there

217

is still a third form of proprietary protection destined to have a significant impact on the other two.

D. PATENT

A legal monopoly for 17 years, giving the owner absolute right over both the idea and the manner of its expression. Would't this make everyone rush to patent software? Why waste time with trade secret and copyright if a patent is so strong? The reason the rush is just a trickle is the length of time, difficulty, and enormous expense (average about $50,000 needed to acquire a patent). The dynamics of the software industry limit the technological edge for any one software product to a very small amount of time, thereby nullifying the effect for any monopoly.   This can be likened, for example, to having a monopoly on the first version of Basic: no one uses it now, so it is useless.   Further, patent protection is designed for machines, not for literary forms of expression (like software). So besides needing speedier protection, software is generally an inappropriate subject for patent protection.

Another problem with the use of the patent device is the cost of defending the already expensive proprietary right. Litigation is always going to be expensive, whether dealing with trade secret or copyright, and patent protection magnifies such expense by a factor of "ten." Limited to the advice of a few specialists qualified to understand that particular field of law, the litigant is confronted with a legal club that is itself a near monopoly. All of which translates into "very expensive talent." Perhaps more importantly, the record shows that most patent claims fail. This indicates a significant probability that after spending much time and money, the patent owner will lose in the end. This is a bleak picture, but there are still those who enjoy the quixotic--so patent applications for software have increased.

(1) Qualification: To qualify for a patent application, the software product must be "new" and "non-obvious." Examples of recent software patents can help define those terms. Patent number 4,355,371 corrects misspelled words. It uses a dictionary to match words based on their likelihood of being the correct version. The "newness" feature of this software product is that whole words are used for the matching process, instead of the old "single letter" methods. The non-obvious characteristic is that is was unexpected--a quantum leap in technology, advancing the state of the art.

In the case of Patent number 4,309,756, the software feature patented permits conversion from source to object code in a single step. Again, the newness of that feature was that all previous technology used several steps. The non-obvious characteristic was that because it was unexpected (could not be foreseen), it advanced the state of such technology.

Those two examples define "newness" as a feature of the software product which indicated an advancement over existing technology that performs the same process. The spelling program used whole words instead of separate letters. The compiler program converted with one instead of several steps. The "non-obvious" characteristic of those examples is that the unexpected technological leap inherent in each of those inventions added to the level of technology for their particular process.

To know if a particular software product is new, one must research existing software patents and technical literature. Otherwise, the result may be an attempt to patent a process or methodology that already exists, leading to failure after significant expenditure of time and money.

(2). Filing: Once satisfied that the software product's features are "new", the filing must show that it is also non-obvious. It must show, in effect, that the software feature benefits technological development because a person familiar with the existing methodology or process could not foresee the invention's new technological level. Filing is an expensive procedure, requiring three steps: a body of text called specifications, a set of drawings, and a claim.

* The specifications are a printed text describing the invention's technological field and the problems solved. It emphasizes the advantages arising from use of the invention, such as reduced cost and improved productivity.

* The drawings describe how the invention functions. A flow chart is often used to describe the invention's underlying principal by detailing the software's methodology and arithmetical figures.

* The claim is a word picture that defines the invention. It describes exactly what the monopoly (patent) protects (in effect, what the public cannot use without a license from the patent owner).

(3). <u>Completion</u>: Completion of the entire process may take months. After the patent office accepts a software program with "patentable" features, the owner may license others to use that product in return for royalties. The problem, of course, is infringement. There is always someone out there who will come up with the same, or a variation of the same, process. The consequence is a long, tedious and expensive litigation battle. If the court finds the variation to be significantly different, it will rule against the patent owner--denying infringement. The probability of such occurence is significant, because of courts' inclination to prevent restraint on the migration of ideas. (There is a judicial tendency to encourage movement of ideas from older to newer technology.) The result: the software patent owner's probability of proving infringement is hardly overwhelming.

An interview with Stephen Kahn, Esq. follows. Although different from that expressed by this author, Mr. Kahn's point of view is nevertheless relevant to the importance of choosing the form of intellectual property protection most appropriate for the owner's/distributor's business needs.

Stephen D. Kahn is a partner in the New York City law firm of Davis, Hoxies, Faithfull 'b Hapgood which specializes in all areas of intellectual property law. Mr. Kahn received his B.E. degree with Highest Honors from Yale University in 1964 and his L.L.B. degree from Yale Law School in 1968. He was a patent attorney with Bell Telephone Laboratories in 1968 and 1969 and has practiced law at Davis Hoxie since that time.

SOFTWARE PROTECTION BY PATENTS
(Interview with Stephen D. Kahn)

Q1. What is patentable about software?

A1. Under our United States patent law, only certain types of inventions are patentable subject matter. Among these types, defined in the federal Patent Act, are "processes" and "machines." Until 1981, it was generally thought, even by patent lawyers, that software was not a machine or a process as those terms are defined in the Act, and therefore that software could not be patented. The truth, even before 1981, was neither so simple nor so bleak.

Some attorneys involved in protecting computer-related inventions recognized many years earlier that this was an over-simplification. They knew even then that patent applications for software inventions could be successfully steered through the Patent Office if they were drafted properly in the first place. In 1981, the Supreme Court made this knowledge public in two decisions upholding the patentability of software related inventions.

The problem in obtaining patent protection for software had always been limited to patenting software

223

standing by itself. Programs in that form look like alternates to procedures that can be accomplished by a person using pencil and paper, and therefore do not look like patentable subject matter. That is, a program written on a sheet of paper does not look like a machine or a process.

However, when software is installed on a computer and put to use, the combination of the computer and the software is certainly a machine, and certainly performs a process. It may be a word processing machine, a CAD/CAM machine, a video game machine or a rubber curing machine, depending on the nature of the software. Whether it is recording this article as I write it, designing a complex three-dimensional part, entertaining my daughter, or controlling a rubber molding operation, it is surely performing a process.

This insight has always been the key to patent protection for software. The Supreme Court in 1981 adopted this form of analysis and effectively revealed the secret to all who cared to listen. The Supreme Court, and other courts following its lead, have evolved a test for patentability of software. The test asks whether the invention claimed in the patent application as a whole is directed to merely a mathematical operation (in which case it is not patentable) or whether it is directed to an industrial machine or process using a mathematical operation (in which case it passes the test and is patentable). While programs themselves have never been legally proper subject matter for patent protection, software that causes a computer to act in some fashion or perform some function may now clearly be protected, in conjunction with the computer, by a patent. To a significant degree, it is all in the drafting!

This result should not be surprising. A patent application is not a simple form, like a copyright registration form, to be filled out by the inventor. It is a complex legal document that should be carefully planned and executed by an attorney, in close collaboration with the inventor. It should be reviewed carefully by the inventor before filing to insure that it is directed to the meaningful aspect of his/her invention. With software, there is often some machine manipulation, some clever interaction among the computer's components being made in the course of executing the program, and this feature may be the subject of a valid, and extremely valuable, patent.

This last point needs to be stressed. There is no

reason to assume that the entire program must be patentable as an overall entity. Far from it. As we will see later, there are reasons for hoping for the opposite situation. All it takes is one non-obvious feature; a particular subroutine that provides a shortcut, a nifty use of the storage capacity of a microprocessor, etc. That is what the patent should cover.

Such a patent could have significant value, since it would protect not only the relatively inexpensive software, but also the computer itself, in combination with the software. Moreover, it would protect that combination no matter what overall activities were being performed, whether word processing, game playing, machine design or rubber molding. In other words, the patented combination of software-plus-computer could not be made, used or sold by others without the patent owner's permission for a period of 17 years from the date the patent issued, no matter what else they were having their computer do.

Q2. Due to the limited market window for most software products why would it make sense for a vendor to consider the expense and uncertainties of obtaining a patent?

A2.   A good question, and one that should probably be asked much more often by decision-makers in many areas of technology, not just software.

In many cases, patent protection makes no sense for a software product for exactly the reason implied in the question.   Obtaining a patent takes a minimum of 12 months from the date of filing and often twice that time.   If the invention is not likely to have economic value for more than a year, a patent would be an expensive ego builder to hang on the wall and get dusty.

In addition, a patent is far more expensive to obtain than is a copyright or trade secret, and a patent can be held invalid by a court at the end of an expensive, time-consuming litigation if it is not carefully drafted or if the invention turns out not to be new.

Despite these negative features, patents sometimes make a great deal of sense for software products.   A patent gives its owner the right to exclude all others from making, using or selling the patented invention for 17 years.   Patents have these other advantages over the other forms of protection:

(1) Unlike copyright or trade secrecy, patents protect against independent creation.

This means that no person can market a program containing the patented feature, even if they can prove beyond any doubt that they developed it in total ignorance of your product.

(2) Unlike trade secret protection, patent protection is not lost by public disclosure of the patented thing.

Disclosures of the type that are fatal to trade secret status are totally irrevelant to patent validity. If the software product will be widely marketed, trade secrecy may not protect it. (Label licenses - the notices appearing through the shrink wrap on software products that say in large print "Read This Before Opening" and go on to say in small print that the $39.95 program is a trade secret and by opening the wrap you agree to keep it secret - may not be enforceable. No one knows yet for sure.) Therefore, patent protection may offer the only alternative.

(3) Unlike copyrights, patents protect ideas. Your competitor is free to analyze your program to learn

its ideas whether it is protected by patent or copyright. However, your competitor cannot then recode those ideas into a different expression, if your program is patented. That would still constitute infringement of your patent. On the other hand, the competitor can do exactly this, with impunity, if your program is only protected by copyright.

These features of patent law demonstrate why it is, in some instances, the best way to protect a software related invention. If the invention--and remember, it need not be the whole program, just a piece of it will do--appears to have usefulness in other applications that may be marketable for years, patent protection may be invaluable.

A current example is the Merrill Lynch patent on its Cash Management Account, a patent now in litigation in the Delaware district court. Imagine the economic value of that patent, which could prevent any entity other than Merrill Lynch from marketing a service combining a brokerage account with a checking account-- for 17 years!

The "bottom line" answer to this question is: in the right circumstances, patent protection may be worth seeking. Not always, not usually, but sometimes.

Q3. What insight can you provide to a software vendor to assist in determining whether trade secret, copyright or patent would be the best proprietary device for protecting a software product?

A3. The first insight is that competent assistance can best be given by an attorney versed in all forms of intellectual property protection. This is not an advertisement for patent attorneys; it is a statement of fact. An attorney not familiar with all species of protection will not be able to look at the problem from all perspectives.

Once adequate counsel is involved, the method of distribution must be considered.

Trade secrecy depends on the ability of the distributer to attach permanent strings to each copy of the software he/she distributes. If strings cannot be kept in place, trade secret status is likely to be lost. This has been discussed above. Label licenses on microcomputer software represent the software companies' last hope of trade secret protection for their code, and the enforceability of such licenses is very much in doubt. If you are going to mass market your product, I recommend that you not place all your eggs in the trade secret basket.

Copyright is always available, and can coexist with either or both of patent or trade secret protection. Whichever form of additional protection you choose to adopt, or even if you choose neither, copyright notices should be placed on your software products. There is nothing inconsistent any more about placing a copyright notice on material which is also considered to be a trade secret. (Note I did not say copyright registration should immediately be sought. There is a substantial legal question whether trade secret status remains intact once a copyright registration is obtained. Since copyright registration can be obtained long after copyright notices are placed on the software, it is probably better in most cases not to register right away, at least until the law is clarified. As a general proposition you need register only before suing someone for infringement. What delay costs you is the monetary award you can receive after winning an infringement suit.)

In addition to distribution methods, the proprietor must weigh the ability of competitors to evade

231

copyright by analyzing the software to ascertain its ideas and then recode the ideas into a noninfringing expression. Copyright, it will be remembered, does not protect an idea; a patent does.

Finally, the owner must decide in cool, unemotional fashion how valuable is the software, how unique in technical terms as opposed to marketing terms,and how long are its individual features likely to have importance. Patent protection should not lightly be sought unless its up-front costs appear justified.

Finally, having analyzed the merits and limits of each form of intellectual property protection, the proprietor should consider how they may blend together to maximize his protection. It is possible, in the right circumstances, to use all three forms of protection to cover a software product. Here is how that might work.

A patent application might be filed on a portion of the product, in the context of a particular machine or process in which it is used. As to that portion of the program, the patent laws require that a good faith disclosure be made. However, the current law does not require that the lines of code actually used be disclosed. That is considered to be something people in the field can readily add themselves.

Therefore, if the product is marketed in a way that protects its trade secret nature, for example, through the use of written licenses, then all other aspects of the program, that is, all aspects not part of the disclosure of your patent application, remain secret. In addition, a copyright notice can be placed on the product, preserving that bundle of rights as well.

One other point should be made. Patent applications remain secret until the day a patent issues. If circumstances change during the time the application is pending such that you would prefer maintainence of secrecy to obtaining a patent, the application can be abandoned at any time until the day the patent is granted.

Q4. How do you see the law of intellectual property (trade secret, copyright or patent) changing to meet the proprietary needs of the software industry?

A4. Slowly! Legal systems always change slowly. That is their nature and, usually, one of their virtues. Legal means for protecting intellectual property have a particuarly tough row to hoe, since technology by its very nature is always evolving.

The first reaction of the legal system to new technology is to shoehorn its characteristics into existing legal frameworks. That is what happened over the last decade with computer software, as government agencies and courts struggled to apply the terms "machine" and "process" to sequences of 1s and 0s that made machines perform astounding feats. That is what is just now beginning to happen with biotechnology.

If it becomes clear that the existing systems do not adequately protect the new technology, then pressure for change begins to be felt. Our federal system makes change in this area complex to carry out, because trade secrecy is part of state, and not federal law, but copyright and patent are exclusively federal!

Pressure for legal recognition of the special needs of the computer industry to date has been exerted mainly on Congress. As a result of that pressure, it appears likely that a bill granting a form of copyright protection to semiconductor chip masks will pass in 1984 or more likely in 1985. This legislation will make illegal the copying of chip masks, a form of competition that has proved impossible to stop by existing legal means.

Once "mask works," as this bill refers to them, are clearly protected by law, the software industry may well begin to shape its technology to the legal framework. It will probably become more common to find software marketed in ROM cartridges rather than on disks. A strange case of law directing technology! (2) (Copyright 1984 Stephen D. Kahn).

E. <u>Summary</u> - <u>Preserving</u> <u>Ownership</u>

We have discussed the strengths and weaknesses of the proprietary devices used by the software industry to protect new technological development. Trade secret, copyright and patent have been presented so that a non-lawyer can determine which device is most appropriate for a particular product.

The next Chapter will describe the threat of computer crime in the software industry and how individuals can be caught in the ever-tightening net of "action-reaction."

FOOTNOTES

(1) <u>IBM's Guidelines to Employee Privacy</u>, Harvard Business
Review, 1976.

(2) <u>Software Protection by Patents</u>, Stephen D. Kahn, March 25,
1984.

CHAPTER IV
COMPUTER CRIME: "THE NEW MENACE"

A. INTRODUCTION

Within less than a second, a command can direct a computer 3000 miles away to reroute the destination of millions in corporate funds. Another touch, and the transaction is erased. A perfect crime. Both the money and the trail have disappeared in an electronic flicker. Fiction? The corporation that lost $10 million dollars in that transaction wished that it had been fiction! Action by the emblezzler, who is still roaming free and untraced, exemplifies why computer crime has become big business. Over $300 million dollars per year and growing--but that is only the reported thefts. The figure does not include the loss of data, extortion, invasion of privacy, and other offences hidden from the public by victims' fear of disclosure.

Nature: Crime is a crime is a crime! Whether by computer or by hammer, taking another's property without permission, distorting data to create a false perception, or using information to compel another to act against self-interest are all criminal acts. The result is the same; only the technology differs--and its use does not require a genius I.Q. A generation of computer-literate individuals has grown up versed in the new technology. The democratization of information-processing skills

237

has enhanced the opportunity for abuse by a factor of ten. Virtually anyone with a modicum of skill or interest can tap into a line, fiddle with a code or circumvent access restrictions. Add the emphasis on creativity fostered by an educational system fascinated with problem-solving--and the questions of when "play" becomes "abuse" grows murky. Educators have confused the situation by teaching problem-solving as an end in itself. The technician's perception has been narrowed to solving the technological riddle. Ethics, morals, and even law, become irrelevant in the relentless task of finding technical solutions. The result: people who would never have stolen a dime, who would be shocked by acts of violence, who would never have the slightest inclination to hurt anyone else, use technology in an unrestrained and often unprincipled manner. They have no compunction about using someone else's computer facilities to operate a clandestine business, embezzle money, distort data, or just talk to their friends. So the problem is one of confusion: how to understand that the abuse of technology is not just "Dungeons and Dragons" (creativity at play), but, rather, acts of serious consequence that may cause injury, loss, or disruption - that such abuse is, in effect, a crime. The following examples should help resolve that ambiguity by illustrating the types of acts that should be considered computer crime.

238

B.   THE NATURE OF COMPUTER CRIME

Embezzlement: This tops the list. It is as if the computer
was created just for that particular crime. Everyone, from
little old ladies to master criminals, dabble in the art of
stealing from employers. A natural ally, computers permit
manipulation of numbers far more effectively than the fabled
little old bookkeeper who never took a vacation (Ah, the price of
dedication!). The Wells Fargo Bank case is a classic example. A
reported $21.3 million dollars looted. Probably the largest such
computer crime in history. Committed by a trusted bank employee
and two co-conspirators who used a pirated code to manipulate the
computer debit and credit files at the same branch. By posting a
credit covering the funds withdrawn by an accomplice, the bank's
computer validated the false transaction made at that branch. To
accomplish this embezzlement the "trusted" employee, who had an
intimate knowledge of the bank's system, needed only ten (10)
minutes every fifth working day to complete the posting
manipulation. Caught only by an error in posting (otherwise it
could have continued indefinitely), the scheme quickly unraveled,
but not before most of the money had been spent. The computer
was the key, able to instantaneously juggle accounts validating
false transactions. The pattern which emerges shows a trusted
employee with intimate knowledge of the system who required only
a minimal amount of time to use the computer to fool itself.
This same pattern was repeated by hospital employees who

programmed an in-house computer which they operated to validate payment for false invoices to a dummy corporation they controlled. Again, audit checks were lax, supervision non-existent, and employees had carte blanche to seize a golden opportunity.

As the next example illustrates, however, an intimate knowledge of the system is not essential in order to manipulate the computer. A data processing employee programmed the computer of a major oil company to make false lease payments to his wife. By assigning her an alphanumeric code close to the codes used for other recipients, the computer was "fooled" into authorizing payment. Again, this scheme was caught only by a fluke audit--but it was simplicity itself to maintain. The "golden opportunity" was created by lack of supervision and control over access to the source code. All the employee had to do was "be there." This low level of security allowed him to play with the coding, find the right formula, and then create his own account.

Clearly, all of the above cases are crimes. Using technology to steal money. The frightening aspect of such crimes is not the act, but the victims' reactions. Instead of outrage there is fear that the public will lose faith in the victim's credibility after learning that its computer system's security had been penetrated. For that reason, even if discovered, most such embezzlers are not convicted. Indeed, as illustrated by another oil company, many such "errant" employees are rewarded. Two individuals worked as programmers for the refinery owned by a major oil company. They had access to the program that authorized payment for products and services purchased by that refinery. Creating their own dummy corporation, they inserted its name into the computer program, authorizing payment for invoices. In effect, they sold the refinery back its own inventory. When the crime was caught by a fluke audit, the oil company decided that news of such embezzlement could damage its credibility. With a promise that they would use their skills to improve security ("it takes a thief to catch a thief"), the two programmers were promoted and charged with designing security support programs. The formula of corporate cover-up used by that refinery to avoid potentially damaging "publicity" has been followed by large numbers of business entities sensitive to their public image. Result, no one really knows the extent of such crimes. What is worse, the crime of embezzlement has been expanded to include the taking of computer time or wrongfully accessing data processing information banks. Illustrative is the saga of two individuals who were separately hired as programmers by a food wholesaler which was expanding its data processing facilities. These individuals were secretly the principals of a service bureau that had contracted to process the data of local businesses, which included a competitor of the food wholesaler. To illicitly operate their business, while using the food wholesaler's data processing facilities, they would bar other employees from the data processing room prior to processing their client's data on the employer's CPU. Such lack of subtlety tends to attract interest, even from the densest of victims. An investigation was launched, resulting in the conviction of those individuals, who saw nothing wrong with the activities. As they viewed the situation, the computer was sitting there, idle; and since no one was hurt, what was the harm? Never mind that the DP facility belonged to someone else and was being used in an unauthorized manner to run a separate business that aided competitors. The programmers did not consider that circumstance. All they saw was the problem: how to use that idle data processing time profitably.

As for the employer, one might ask why didn't such strange behavior--locking other employees out of the computer room-- attract immediate interest instead of a slow build-up of attention over the course of several months. The answer was startling. Management was not interested. Its focus was on marketing; anything else was secondary. Not an unusual perception for businesses, whether small or large. Time is money, and the supervising of facilities is often considered more costly than it is worth. For that reason, security considerations did not merit management's attention. Underlying this lack of interest was the perception that the information processed was not valuable. Management just did not understand the value of the computer facility or the information it

242

processed. Considerable discussion was needed first to convince management that unauthorized use of computer facilities was "stealing computer time." What finally moved this management group to action was the fact that the two programmers were processing data for a competitor. As the saying goes: "Whatever turns you on!"

Courts, however, have demonstrated an understanding that unauthorized use of DP facilities by employees is a crime. Computerworld, in its February 20, 1984 issue, reported that an Indiana Appeals Court ruled that a former computer programmer for the Indianapolis Department of planning and Zoning must face sentencing for using the city's IBM 3031 computer in connection with his second job of selling a franchised diet product. The programmer's defense attorney likened such activity to using the "office Xerox machine for copying a recipe." But the Appellate Court agreed with the prosecutor that computer services are a large part of the national economy, and that since the use of computer time is a service for which money is paid, it is a property. In essence, the Court held that the defendant had stolen property (computer time) belonging to his employer.

In another example with a twist, computer information was wrongfully taken and used. It seems that a deputy sheriff with access to the county computer data bank decided to join a private investigator without relinquishing his password to the

County Police District data bank. He made copies of the passwords used by his former colleagues in case his was terminated. By accessing that facility after leaving his position as deputy sheriff, he began to establish a reputation for solving client problems. Events looked rosy until he used the password belonging to a former colleague who was simultaneously using that same access code. Suspicious, the computer center began investigation and unearthed the thievery-- nipping a "brilliant career" in the bud. As it turned out, the computer center was lax on security, employing almost no audit trails, supervision, or monitoring of access by end-users. Result, a golden opportunity was created to wrongfully access the information stored in that data bank. The interesting twist in this case is that the former deputy sheriff did not wait until he was terminated before using the data bank to further his career as a private investigator. While working at his job, he would pass information to his fellow private investigator, and, of course, he continued that activity after termination. The court held that the information taken was property and that its unauthorized use was an act of theft.

These examples show that technology has been used by employees to embezzle money, steal computer time and data as well as to operate a clandestine business using the employer's CPU. In virtually all those cases the defendants argued that no one was hurt. The computer was sitting there--idle--or the information was used to pursue criminals. Even the bank employees argued that they helped their employer tighten security, thereby improving credibility. The latter justification is like saying that a mugging victium shouldn't complain because he'll be better prepared the next time it happens. It is curious that the victims of crimes involving theft of computer time or data often don't complain. These same people would be outraged if their cars were stolen, but have shown little concern about the theft of computer time or data-- because the theft is generally unseen. For that reason, complaints are rare. After all, it is unusual to find programmers brazen enough to lock workers out of the DP facility in order to operate their clandestine service bureau.

Theft: Number two on the criminal hit parade is theft: A person (generally not an employee) using technology to con, steal or intimidate. The most common culprit is the consultant who, like an employee, enjoys a position of trust with access to confidential information. Take the consultant who decided to reprogram a CPU to hide the theft of $100,000. Hired to create an accounts payable and general ledger program, the consultant (as the guru) worked without supervision. Since no one in management had any idea what the consultant was doing, they could not supervise, even if they thought it was necessary. Basically, they abrogated their obligation to control, relying on the crutch labelled "lack of expertise." As the consultatnt worked on developing those programs, he also took pains to insure extra compensation by coding the system to ignore checks made payable to fictitious employees, who he endorsed for cash. This activity continued for several months until a new accountant noticed lots of "extra paper" floating around. The "paper" was traced to the consultant, who confessed--but not before the money had been spent. As part of his sentence he had to "debug" the system, but this time he did his work under supervision.

Again, a clear case of trust betrayed. A person placed in an unsupervised situation is given a golden opportunity to make a "few extra dollars that no one will ever miss" (said the consultant). Expertise relied upon to solve problems apparently causes management to default on supervision. Such was the situation for another consultant, who used that opportunity to blackmail his client. Working for a major high-tech company on one portion of a secret formula designed to improve the surface coating for floppy disks, he was able to surreptitiously acquire the other elements of that formula. Apparently gathering that information proved easy. Poor security and a friendly working atmosphere (everyone is a colleague), made the formula elements accessable without any real difficulty. After he put all the pieces together, proof was sent to the vice president in charge of the project that the complete formula was known, along with a demand for one million dollars. The threat was that he would sell the formula to the Japanese. Payment arrangements for transfer of funds were settled, and the consultant then found himself caught with both funds and formula by the FBI, which had staked out the drop. Again the pattern: management, relying on expertise, fails to supervise (ostensibly because it doesn't have the knowledge needed to understand the consultant's activity) thereby providing a golden opportunity to wrongfully use or take technology.

Private individuals often hide their heads in the sand when it comes to dealing with technology. Lack of inquiry provides an opportunity for bunko artists to hide behind the computer mystique while collecting money from a gullible public. The same people who brought you the old pyramid schemes now provide a computerized version that dazzles with promises of opportunity. Take the scheme to match potential buyers with businesses for sale. Using computers, the scam promised clients interested in selling businesses that they could match them with buyers within less than a year. In fact only one business out of more than 2,000 was sold through that computerized system. The prosecution found that instead of using the fees collected to buy ads in national publications the money went for airplanes and luxury cars. There may be no accounting for tastes but there should be an accounting to those who invested money in computerized mystique. In this case, facination with computer mystique cost the public (mostly business owners) over $4 million dollars. As with the company that found itself being blackmailed, those business owners failed to ask any questions, because they were relying on "experts." Clearly, the above examples show that lack of accountability permits use of the new technology to steal, extort or defraud.

Intrusion--Technological Tresspass: Probably one of the most malicious acts is entering a data base and modifying or distorting information. A California college student found he was able to enter a university's research data base. Modifying the files he caused the loss of hundreds of thousands of dollars in research time. In addition, future projects that depended on the lost information were imperiled. Adding insult to injury, the student left messages in the files indicating his presence and mocking the system's security. Arrested for destroying university property the student could not understand all the fuss. After all, he was just playing; didn't mean any harm, and had merely applied the lessons taught by that university in creatively using his expertise. He failed to understand the legal and ethical limits on the creative use of that expertise, a fault attributable to those who did the educating. As a college professor once remarked to this author, creativity should be encouraged with unlimited problem-solving. Did that mean a total lack of respect for laws, ethics and morality? The professor did not understand the relationship between technological tools and the society in which those tools are applied. This blind spot caused by the narrow focus on problem solving was also apparent in the Dalton School case where students at that institution broke the code of a major business organization's data bank, gained access and "hacked around." The school administrators were certain that the appearance of the FBI and a good "talking to" would prevent any further "misadventures." They treated the episode as exercise without accountability for damage. The result was that one of the students was again caught trying to wrongfully access a data bank. His "gamesmanship" attitude precluded any thought about the consequences suffered by the victim whose data bank was abused. Apparently, the attitude of most educators is akin to teaching someone how to shoot without worrying who gets hit by the bullet. This attitude was exemplified by the "414's," a student group who used common carrier computer networks to enter such august data banks as Los Alamos Research Laboratories or Sloan Kettering (where they monitored patient information). When caught, the students argued "no harm done." Sure, they should not have been there but, as they said, "what the hey, it's all in fun!". Again, the attitude of gamesmanship. No accountability, because it is a creative exercise that makes it right to trespass and destroy information. In another example, that attitude almost led to death. A 14-year-old was playing with a Hewlett-Packard microcomputer when, using a modem (communication device), he was able to tap into the data bank of a hospital. Thinking himself clever, he began to change patient information, such as allergic reactions, history, prognosis, etc. At the same time, a physician relying on that information in the hospital's data bank prescribed a drug for a certain patient which he believed (based on that history) would not cause an allergic reaction. While on the way to administer that dosage the hospital's technician was intercepted by the same, visibly agitated, doctor who learned that the hospital's records were unreliable. Apparently a computer technican noticed irregularties in the data bank concerning a number of patients and was able to flag procedures involving those computerized files. Had the patient been given that drug (at the prescribed dosage) it would have caused a life-threatening allergic reaction. A close call, but again the student argued "no harm done." The fact that someone's life was threatened did not appear to be of interest, since the student was merely "solving problems." Trespassing on property, by entering someone's data bank is like entering someone's home without permission. The trespasser doesn't belong there and, the belief that its "all in fun" doesn't dilute the legal and moral consequences of that act. Using the new technology to trespass creates enormous potential for harm. As demonstrated by the example involving the hospital, there could be instances where tampering with information could be life-threatening. Beyond that, the destruction of business or government records (such as at Los Alamos) could have severe repercussions affecting national security, which is certainly not a laughing matter. Hopefully, educators will recognize that the enormous potential of computer intrusion for harming lives, businesses or national security is a sufficient reason to teach accountability in conjunction with problem-solving. To assist in that recognition process, courts have begun to slap computer intruders with stiff fines and jail sentences. Take the case of the California "phone freak" who wreaked havoc with Pacific Telephone Company's system. Using a microcomputer and modem, this person entered the telephone company's CPU and altered key data such as billing records and stop orders. His ultimate goal was to cause such havoc as to shut down the company, a circumstance that would have distressed millions of users. In addition, with the help of some fellow phone freaks, he entered a leasing company's CPU and destroyed the inventory information of its subsidiary, literally shutting down that company. Some fun! Millions in damages--a major leasing company virtually put out of business--all because of the challenge to "beat the system." The court recognized the perverse nature of the phone freak's sense of humor and sentenced him to a lengthy jail term so he could think about the destruction he caused. More such jail terms are in the offing as courts recognize that computer time and information stored in computerized files are property to be protected by law.

Unless educators teach accountability along with technology, the severity of incidents involving theft, intrusion, or destruction of information will increase the new technology's social cost, resulting in the need for greater control by government.

<u>The</u> <u>Gray</u> <u>Market--Counterfeiting</u> <u>Computer</u> <u>Products</u>: It doesn't require a "whiz kid" to steal a chip, but technical skills are necessary to duplicate such a product. Counterfeit products are common in the computer industry. For example, replicating the mask on a silicon chip requires technological skills as well as overhead, but the demand is such that the cost is worth the effort. The risk is minimal, since most buyers are happy to get the chips quickly, at a lower than market price. A major electronic firm that began purchasing hundreds of chips from a small supplier at lower than market price is an example. The chips were always paid for in cash, and shipments were generally made after most employees had left. Eventually, the supplier was found to be a counterfeiter. When questioned, however, the major electronics firm denied any knowledge or even suspicion that the chips were counterfeit. A curious denial, because they admitted that the chips were normally hard to get and that cash payments for nighttime deliveries were rare. Clearly, the gray market for countfeit goods requires willing buyers unwilling to ask questions. When products like computer chips are hard to get, the silence of buyers can be deafening. As one vice president for a major hardware vendor said, "who would quibble about the purchase of chips at half the market price and at a delivery frequency faster than available from the chip's original manufacturer?" Defenders of counterfeiting operations assert that the public benefits because market scarcity is often designed by the manufacturer to keep prices

artificially high. A classic example of that argument is the price of Apple IIe products, that dropped drastically because of competition from "knock-offs" such as the "Pineapple or Orange," made in Taiwan. The other side is that knock-offs chill technological development by making it difficult for manufacturers to recoup the costs of product development. This situation reduces manufacturers' willingess to invest in research efforts. The public is also harmed, because many knock-offs are not made under the quality control standards set by the original manufacturer. This results in the production of shoddy goods having higher than usual performance failure rates. In any event, the public is hardly served by the theft and corruption that are the byproducts of counterfeit operations.

Unfortunately, the lack of public interest in knock-offs is matched by an equal disinterest in goods "hot" off the truck. For instance, police were notified of an Apple computer theft ring only when several "amazingly" honest individuals reported that they were approached by people willing to sell them Apple III's for less than $1000. After launching a probe of the Apple manufacturer with the aid of company officials, five Apple employees were arrested. They were accused of stealing over a million dollars worth of Apple III's. Some of the customers for those stolen computers proved to be Hong Kong counterfeiters who would sell knock-offs in the U.S. under names similar to Apple's. Theft of computer products is big business. FBI officials believe that organized crime controls underground theft rings.

One of the most notorious gray markets is the one for software. Virtually everyone at some point in time will make an unauthorized copy of a software product. The real threat is from underground distribution houses that copy thousands of popular software programs and sell them to retailers at cut-rate prices. Those people often reduce their orders from legitimate distributors, while selling the counterfeit at the original's price, making an enormous profit. This type of activity is extremely difficult to curb, because the buyer gains as much as the counterfeiter.

In general, the gray market for knock-offs and stolen computer products is big business. Curbing it requires a willingness by individuals to avoid being corrupted through access to cheap counterfeits or stolen goods. Until the public recognizes that such pervasive corruption is symptomatic of a widespread disinterest in responsibility for the abuse of technology, the evolution of new computer products will reflect the cost of computer crime.

Patterns: What, then, is the nature of computer crime? As the above examples illustrate, it involves the use of technology to steal, distort or destroy. From manipulating computers to cover embezzlement or theft, to the modification or destruction of computerized information fields, the list of innovative methods for wrongfully using technology is endless. A pattern, however, does emerge:

a) Trust: Employees, former employees or outside experts, such as consultants, are often the principal villains. The key to their opportunity is trust. A high degree of confidence is vested in employees, particularly senior personnel, who process information or operate computer systems. Such trust is also placed in outside experts who are relied upon to cure problems or create systems using their superior technical knowledge. In effect, this high degree of trust precludes follow-up and supervision, because management reasons that since it doesn't understand the employee's (or consultant's) technical decision, there is no basis for effective supervision. Accordingly, opportunity is created for the embezzlement of funds, computer time, or data.

b) Carelessness: Following trust in the pattern is carelessness. Again, management's abrogation of its supervision over data processing facilities is like leaving the fox to guard the chickens. Classic is the stolen source code for a major bank's financial applications. All the master codes for each financial application were contained on several reels of magnetic tape that an assistant manager happened to leave on her desk, in plain sight, for several days. You guessed it, one day the tapes disappeared, throwing all financial operations into chaos. The bank found itself unable to control, let alone verify the authenticity of the thousands of varied transactions it normally handles. A nightmare--due to simple carelessness. Technicians generally do not have the broad scope needed to understand the priority of security support. The $21.3 million dollar embezzlement by a trusted system operator could have been avoided if there were tighter audit controls and supervision. The theft of computer time by a university's senior data processing staff (to run their clandestine business) could have been avoided with audits, reporting procedures and closer scrutiny by management. Such internal theft, destruction or abuse of data could have been avoided by implementing, enforcing and monitoring access control procedures.

c) Fear of Technology: Computer mystique still compels senior management to maintain a "hands off" ("it can't happen here") attitude toward operating data processing facilities. Reliance on the "experts," as seen from the above examples, is an open invitation for opportunists to indulge in unauthorized activities ranging from "hacking" to operating an entire business using the employer's data processing facilities. Such overwhelming reliance with its concomitant hands-off approach is a reaction to the mystique generated by such new technology. "I don't understand it, so how can I supervise its operations" goes the plaintive chant of senior management personnel. Abrogating

256

responsibility is not the answer. There is a plethora of audit expertise for sale, able to assist in monitoring the operation of data processing facilities. Numerous reporting procedures are available to help management not only understand data processing operations but curb the opportunity for abuse. All it requires is thought, effort and a willingness to treat the new technology, like any other business tool, with respect and an understanding of potential.

d) The New Technology: The cost of a wire tap has dropped from $20,000 to less than $1,000 in the last several years. Microcomputers with the power of small mainframes have dropped in price to less than $3,000. User-friendly networks have eased access to widely dispersed data banks. The new technology has made it easier to use computer power to steal, distort or destroy. What is worse is that the combination of falling cost and increasing power will escalate opportunitites for such abuse. Recognition of this situation should compel management to employ more security devices to protect against unauthorized use or access. Indeed, paralleling this rise in technological opportunity has been an increase of devices designed to complicate access, trap hackers, garble information or detect intrusion. Remarkably, business organizations have not used protective technology effectively. Only recently have the sales of such devices begun to rise, with users showing an appreciable interest. The reason for the slow uptake is the emphasis by both users and vendors on performance and ease of access. Vendors sell computers on the basis of cost effectiveness. If security devices are used to complicate access and slow response (which does occur) the product's cost effectiveness is diminished. Like being penny wise and pound foolish, this short term perspective of "performance now and don't worry about the future" has exposed data resources to the increased opportunity for wrongful use or access. Vendors blame users for not wanting designed-in security support, much like car makers blamed the public for not wanting seat belts. Unfortunately, most large organizations entrust their data processing facilities to technicians who are interested solely in performance so no compelling motivation exists for vendors to consider designed-in security support. Until business organizations wake up and realize that the best security is that which is designed into the product, the "add-on" protective technology currently used will continue to be expensive, cumbersome and ineffective.

C. SECURITY CONSIDERATIONS: THE PRACTICAL SIDE

The practical side of security considerations is explained by interviews with the following experts:

Frank B. Kemp
Jack Berger
Leonard F. Turi
James M. Doud
Michael A. Daniels
State and Defense Department Officials

Security Considerations Related to
Distributed Processing Installations

Mr. Frank B. Kemp is the Assistant Director of Management Information Systems for Arthur Young. In this position, he is responsible for management of the design and implementation of custom developed and packaged accounting systems that record and report on the activities of the firm. He has fifteen years of management consulting experience. He is a member of the Institute of Management Consultants, and is a Certified Management Consultant (CMC). He has been awarded the Certificate in Data Processing (CDP) by the Institute for Certification of Computer Professionals. In addition, he is recognized by the EDP Auditors Association as a Certified Information Systems Auditor (CISA), having passed that Association's competitive examination.

Q1. As you know, one of the major technological advances for business organizations is distributive processing. Could you explain the nature of distributive processing to a nontechnical audience?

A1. "Distributive processing" describes the joint operation of central and remote data processing facilities, where certain reference files are available and are updated at both the central site and the remote site. These reference files are available to be transmitted from one site to another for consolidation and reporting. "Distributive processing" also implies a high degree of reliance on communications technology, and may often introduce the use of data base technology for data management and control.

Note: At the end of this interview report there are several textbook definitions of "distributive processing." As may be seen, they vary in their description and emphasis.

Q2. If you were to draw on your knowledge to advise a business about to install a distributive processing facility, what types of security considerations would you suggest it include in the planning for such a system?

A2. First, prepare a list of the information that is to be maintained in the system, arranged by the types of users that are expected to reference it. This means all users, whether they are the recipients of reports or the viewers of on-line screens. For example, the classifications may be as rough as: payroll data, receivable data and personnel data.

Next, classify these users as to the level of security that is appropriate, from input clerks through the oversight function of top management.

Finally, match the data to the level of user that is appropriate, and continue to incorporate this system into the requirements of an authorization and monitoring system to accompany the introduction of the system.

Once the above analysis has been performed for the central site, continue with a similar analysis of the information that is planned to be available at the remote sites.

This analysis, mechanical and clerical as it is, will force out into the open considerations such as: who has access to what data, and why. It is guaranteed to take longer than originally expected and to require some tough decisions. However, once it has been completed, the coding of the mechanical rules of a security system will fall into place much more easily than would be the case without this analysis.

Q3. How would you advise such a business to follow through from planning to implementation to assure that the planned security considerations are included in the final system?

A3. Continue to monitor the development of this data security system through management level attention, scheduled progress reports, and periodic verification. (It should be noted that the administration of data security in a distributive processing environment requires management-level attention, and specific attention to detail and follow-up.)

Q4. Do you find that the software and hardware industries generally provide products with designed-in features that support those security considerations? If not, what gaps exist?

A4. Yes, the leading national software and hardware vendors provide products with designed-in features supporting security. However, as in other EDP operations, the responsibility of implementing these features rests with the user management for direction and control. Further, it is management's responsibility to integrate the hardware and software control features in such a manner that legitimate users are not presented with an impossible thicket of passwords, controls and codes standing between them and the productive use of the facility.

Q5. What steps can a busines take to overcome those gaps?

A5. It is management's responsibility to identify and resolve any gaps in the functonality of software and hardware products' security. Resolving these matters includes the task of balancing management's security concerns with the user's concern for a convenient operating environment.

Q6. How can a business that relies on commercial carrier distributive processing networks to transmit or receive information protect its data base from unauthorized intrusion such as that by the infamous "414" Milwaukee Group?

A6. It appears as if the "414" Milwaukee Group and other "hackers" have been successful in cases where there was a lack of management attention to security measures. The facilities that were pentrated by the hackers were large service-bureau centers, with many telecommunications users and apparently neither a dedicated plan for operational monitoring, nor the existence of an active security management approach. This absence of management attention appears to be the case where hackers gain access to the systems through knowledge of the "default" security code--the code most often left in place by the communications or operating system software vendor. If the default value of the security code remained unmodified, then "no one was minding the store" in terms of security management.

To discourage the operation of hackers and to protect a data base from unauthorized intrusion requires an awareness of the potential problem on behalf of management, followed by management commitment to address the problem, backed up by the institution of a continuous security management technology monitoring activity.

Q7. Can those same measures be used to protect against unauthorized entrapment and modification of data during transmission?

A7. While there are certain end-to-end checks that could reveal modification of data while in transmission, it appears as if the high relative cost of these techniques, in relation to their reported incidence of abuse, may not make them appropriate for the average communications user of commercial data carrier services.

In the specific cases where the end-user is especially concerned about this type of abuse, the use of data encryption techniques should be considered.

For the communications vendor, however, the application of controls over unauthorized entrapment and modification of data is appropriate. By providing an assurance of confidentiality and security to users, the communications vendor will be in a position to attract those users who require this service and who are not able to implement these techniques on their own.

Q8. What can a business with a distributive processing facility do to prevent wrongful abuse or even criminal acts by employees?

A8. There are four basic steps:

1. Establish a sound technical environment with the appropriate resources for controlling, monitoring, and enforcing security measures.

2. Set a standard of security measures appropriate to the organization, considering the type of data involved and its users. (This is the "who uses what data" issue described in question #2.)

3. Advise the employees of the standards to be followed, through publication of an explanation of the code of conduct that is expected of them. This code of conduct would be addressed to system development and operations professionals, as well as end users and management personnel.

4. Monitor and enforce the published standard, utilizing all the technical resources available for this purpose, and following the published guidelines, policy and procedures relating to security.

Q9. What effect do you think increased supervision and monitoring would have on employee morale? What steps can be taken to alleviate any such problems?

A9. The mere fact that supervision and monitoring is taking place need not have an adverse effect on employee morale, if the employees have had a degree of participation in the establishment of the standards and if the standards are accompanied by an explanaton of their relevence and involvement in supervision and monitoring will reinforce a recognition that the employees' tasks are important to the organization, and that those tasks should be treated with care and attention. This is the computer-age version of the "Hawthorne-effect": the fact that there is any management attention to a clerical task will tend to increase the level of performance and participation.

Q10. Do you believe that the federal government ought to pass legislation declaring that certain uses of technology are criminal? If so, what type of uses would you want to be classified as crimes?

A10. Yes, it is appropriate that an individual citizen's rights, as originally defined in the Bill of Rights or first 10 amendments to the Constitution, be defined in a new respect to "privacy" in our contemporary computerized society.

Given that a proper definition of these rights can be re-affirmed in this manner, violations of individuals' "privacy" that are subsequently accomplished through abuses of computer technology should be regarded as federal crimes. In this respect, violation of one's rights to privacy through mis-application of computer resources would be a "federal case."

Q11. Going from large businesses to the individual consumer, do you have any advice for those who use commercial local networks (such as bank-by-computer) as to how they can protect themselves against unauthorized access to their confidential information transmitted over those networks?

A11. Currently, individuals really have almost no resources to protect against unauthorized access to their confidential information when it is transmitted over commercial networks. Pending the enactment of federal legislation respecting a standard definition of "privacy," the only realistic recourse of the individual may be to secure a "statement of responsibility" for privacy from the commercial vendor.

Having secured a vendor's "statement" and having incorporated this "statement" as part of the contract, the individual could then expect to seek relief in the courts if the vendor violated the code of conduct outlined in the "statement."

267

Definitions

There seems to be a difference in opinion among professionals as to what distributed processing actually is. The following gives us a look at five definitions from different sources.

From James Martin's, Computer Networks & Distributed Processing: Architectures, Techniques, & Software. He gives us his definition:

"The term distributive processing is used to describe systems with multiple processors. The term has different meanings because processors can be interconnected in many ways for many reasons. For some the term relates to a multiprocessor complex in one location. In its most common usage, however, the word "distributed" implies that the processors are in geographically separate locations. Occasionally, the term is applied to an operation using multiple minicomputers which are not connected at all."

Distributive Processing: Current Practice & Future Developments gives us the following definition:

"Distributive Data Processing is a means of reacting to user demands for more responsive computer systemswhile, at the same time, avoiding the worst excesses of decentralization."

From Down & Taylor's NCC book, <u>Why</u> <u>Distributed</u> <u>Computing</u>, we have:

"A distributed system is one in which there are several autonomous but interacting processors and/or data stores at different geographical locations.

Unless the remote processors used in a distributive system are able to operate for some time independently of any central site, then it is arguable that the system is not truly distributive. This approach would tend to rule out the microprocessor-based displays which are so easily dubbed as 'distributive processing' products by their manufacturers. To have a distributive system requires more than 'intelligent' terminals."

The <u>Computer</u> <u>Literature</u> <u>Index:</u> <u>Annual</u> <u>Cumulation</u> <u>1982</u> gives us this definition:

"Distributive Processing: A system configuration wherein different functions are allocated to different processors within an interconnected network of several processors."

Management Information Systems, by Raymond McLeod, Jr., lists the following definition:

> "Distributive processing is an approach firms use to spread their computing power throughout the organization. They distributed computers, often minis, to regional, area, and branch offices and plants. Distributive Processing requires that more than one information processor be available within the organization and that they be in different locations. The processors can be used in a batch or online manner. According to some, a firm can have a distributive processing system even if the processors are not interconnected in any way. To most, however, the processors must be able to transmit data back and forth, using some type of communication link."

Security Concerns of the Financial-Banking Community

Dr. Jack Berger is Vice President of Citibank and is the Chief of Staff for the Asia Pacific Consumer Businesses, based at corporate headquarters in New York City. Dr. Berger has received Masters and Doctorate Degrees in Chemical Engineering from the University of Illinois. During his career at Citibank, which began in 1971, he has been responsible for large computer systems, developing project management and control systems, standardizing data processing systems for overseas branches, and supervising the development of bank processing systems in Europe and Asia.

Q1.   Define computer crime.

A1.   Computer crime is the use of information management systems and technology to obtain, illegally, money or information or both.   In this regard, the abuse of computers to steal money is but a subset of a larger issue involving the manipulation of information for illegal gain.

Q2.   What have banks done to curb the threat posed by computer crime?

A2.   The issue of providing security for the financial affairs of clients is as old as banking itself.   At the root of financial intermediation services is the implicit understanding that the banker will transact on behalf of the customer with the highest degree of confidentiality.   This was as true before the advent of the computer as it is today, and it will always be so.

The advent of electronic data processing has merely changed the technological emphasis of how the banker goes about providing his clients with the security and confidentiality that is required. During the past generation, banks have refined--and are continuing to refine--the principles by which such safety and security are delivered. These principles include limited and privileged access to data, separation of duties, procedural knowledge access to data, separation of duties, procedural knowledge made available on a need to know basis, and a system of checks and balances that includes various levels of auditing.

As technology changes, the means by which these principles are implemented change as well. The priniciples themselves remain the same, however.

Q3. How do you respond to the argument that the practices and procedures for preventing computer crime are awkward, expensive and reduce cost effectiveness?

A3. You must examine the requirements of the marketplace, and incorporate appropriate responses that reflect the concerns of those who will use your services. No such assessment is complete without also undertaking a practical loss versus the cost of protection. None of the allegations you cite are meaningful in and of themselves; they are all relative. A decade ago, auto exhaust emission control was highly controversial as a cost item. Today, it is axiomatic in auto design. All technical advance undergoes this type of scrutiny in the marketplace, and information processing technology is no exception.

Q4. Can an institution prevent repetition of the $21.3 million embezzlement that occured at Wells Fargo?

A4. Each instance of a defalcation provides an opportunity to review systems and procedures for points of vulnerability. That is why the industry is well served by sharing information on such occurences, despite the fact that they may represent a source of embarrassment to management. Those who are intimately involved in the design of financial transaction processing systems recognize that no system is totally impervious to penetration. One strives to minimize the probability of penetration at a reasonable cost. This instance, along with others, such as the Union Dime defalcation, are the grist for the mill of analysis and evaluation. Each creates its own response from management to strengthen its operating systems so that a repetition will not occur. This is very much in the spirit of analyzing defects that come off a production assembly line. In that spirit, however, there is no guarantee that some different type of subversion will not occur in the future.

Q5.   What effect does employee supervision have on morale (the "they don't trust me so why should I care" syndrome)?

A5.   This is a task that management must address as part of training and communications up and down the line. Few employees in a financial institution will fail to appreciate the need for controls where the handling of money is concerned. Management must understand its responsibility to communicate what it is doing, and why, so that it is clearly understood. If the communication is proper, there is no reason to believe that morale will suffer.

Q6.   With the increased use of electronic funds transfer, what practices and procedures have banks instituted to prevent tap-ins, electronic hi-jacking of funds, or interception and destruction of data in transit?

A6.   This is a very large area, which I can touch on only in a brief manner. Tapping into networks is a problem that goes beyond the concerns of the financial sector alone. All businesses make use of public networks in one way or another. Consequently, the protection of the channels themselves is beyond the scope of financial institutions, and is more properly the concern of the carriers, such as the telephone company.

Financial institutions then concentrate on securing the data that is in transit. This is accomplished by first providing various forms of password protection to limit access to the systems themselves. Second, they make significant use of encryption technology to assure that the information cannot be readily understood by third parties who intercept such data illegitimately. Third, various forms of transaction reconcilement procedures are in place to assure that what is sent by one center is correctly received by another.

Q7. With financial services being expanded to include electronic banking, what have banks done to prevent intercept/modification of data in transit and to protect the confidentiality of the data received?

A7. The answer to this question is much the same as the answer to the previous one. As electronic banking moves the access point to the financial systems out into the user's premises, there is a need to provide more sophisticated and flexible access controls. These are evolving in the marketplace in response to the emerging needs.

Q8. Have vendors been responsive to the security considerations of financial institutions by designing-in security support, or have banks been confronted with the need to buy expensive add-on security support products? What is the disadvantage of "add-on" security support products?

A8. I think this is a mixed area. If you talk to financial institutions, you will find they feel that technology vendors are not moving fast enough. Vendors are likely to indicate that the requirements are not stable enough at this point in time. The cost issue must relate to the prior discussion of risk assessment. The "add-on" technology has the advantage of being isolatable. It can therefore be managed on a need-to-know basis. However, it is probably less flexible when it comes to configuration changes, and therefore more expensive. One can be optimisitc, however, since the pace of change is such that cheaper, and more flexible alternatives are likely to appear in the years to come.

Q9. Are banks concerned about terrorists using "electronic sabotage" to damage data base facilities? If so, what practices and procedures are they implementing to avoid such a threat?

A9. All of the practices and procedures that are useful in preventing the economic abuse of data are equally applicable in preventing abuse of a purely malicious nature, with no economic gain in mind.

Q10. Should the federal government pass a computer crime bill? If so, what types of crimes should be federalized, and why?

A10. On the face of it, it does not appear that incremental legislation would be required. The reason is that computer is a means, and not an end. Illegal appropriation of funds is theft, or larceny, whether it is accomplished by pointing a gun at a bank teller, or defrauding a bank by subverting an electronic transfer.

Stealing trade secrets by tapping a data base is a form of breaking and entering that is fundamentally no different than entering an office by stealth and stealing blueprints.

I believe that the legislators need to examine these types of analogies with the assistance of informed technical experts to determine the degree to which we are dealing with something that the law has not already anticipated.

Security Problems Facing Small and Medium-Sized Businesses Desiring to Automate

Mr. Leonard F. Turi has degrees in Architecture, Business Administration and Law. He was awarded a Certificate in Data Processing (CDP) from the Institute for Certification of Computer Professionals after passing that association's competitive examination. Mr. Turi has accumulated over 23 years of experience involving management consulting, marketing, sales, computer technology, law, architecture and education. He is the Founder, Chairman of the Board, President and Chief Executive officer of TMS Technical Marketing Services, Inc., with offices in New York City and New Jersey. Mr. Turi is the author of Mini/Micro Computers - A How-To Book On Evaluation, Selection and Contracting: The Handbook Of Evaluation And Selection Of Agency Computer System; and A Quick Look At Database Technology. He was a co-author of Privacy Legislation - Trends And Impact On Computerized Information.

Q1. How would you define a small business?

A1. The United States Department of Commerce and The United States Small Business Administration have definitions for a Small Business based upon the number of persons employed and sales revenue. My definition is similarly based but further qualified to encompass computer piracy and privacy considerations.

A company, by my definition, with less than 100 employees and/or 20 million in sales revenues would be considered a small business. However, if that "small business" happened to use a computer system that had a centralized multi-company, multi-user, multi-state, etc., database on a large mainframe computer system accessible by many large and small companies via a timesharing network, I would classify that "small business" as a "large piracy and privacy risk company".

Q2.   What information would such a business have that is worth stealing?

A2.   Pricing, personnel, product, software, schedules, customer lists, tax data, sales, marketing, etc.--or, essentially, all the business services functions that are represented by the nature of the organization's data.

Q3.   What other types of computer crimes could be committed against a small business?

A3.   In addition to crimes involving the theft of corporate data, I envision numerous crimes involving "data diddling," i.e. falsifying records.

Q4.   Will you describe incidents that you know of in which small businesses have been victimized by wrongful use of computer technology?

A4.   One instance I know of is a small hardware supply store that had its computer system accessed by a competitor that

279

used confidential price, product and profit data to compete unfairly.

Q5. What steps should a small business take to protect itself against the type of computer crimes you describe above?

A5. A security plan should be developed that will include personnel training and the employment of computer hardware and software, encryption devices, password and user access techniques.

Q6. How do you respond to the argument that implementing those steps adds cost and slows response time, thereby reducing a system's cost effectiveness?

A6. That is an erroneous argument. The added cost can be insignificant compared with the cost that can result from computer crime involving the theft or misuse of corporate information. The response time and cost effectiveness degregation is negligible. We are talking about the potentital loss of nanoseconds, microseconds, or, at most, seconds of computer time and delayed access.

Q7.   Many small businesses belong to trade associations. How can such associations help their members protect themselves against computer crime?

A7.   By instituting a COMPUTER USERS GROUP, which among other things, would establish a COMPUTER CRIME, PRIVACY, PIRACY, policy statement, education program, newsletters and special interest group panels.

Q8.   In hiring a consultant such as yourself to create or modify a system for a small business, what questions should be asked to determine credibility?

A8.   The questions should be directed to establish the consultant's credentials in the areas of business, law, computer technology and education.   Specific questions would vary, depending upon the industry, computer system, number of users and location of business enterprise.

Q9.   What precautions should be taken in dealing with consultants to avoid providing a "golden opportunity"?

A9.   Customer and character reference checks should be made, limited access to confidential data should be ensured, and no one consultant should have knowledge of the overall security plan and its individual components.

Q10. How does a small business impose practices and the procedures you described without damaging employee morale?

A10. By impressing upon the employees that the security program is designed to protect their company jobs, not only from internal but also from external abuse.

Q11. What type of laws would be helpful to mitigate the threat of computer crime found by small business?

A11. Laws that would stipulate computer system safeguards that vendors would be required to incorporate in the products they sell. This would be something like the regulations aimed at auto safety. Laws are also needed to impose criminal sentences and civil damages awards.

The Vendor's View of The Security Market

Now, for a somewhat different perspective, this author interviewed Mr. James M. Dowd, Chairman of the Board, President and Chief Executive Officer of Design Systems Inc., a computer systems consulting and software company with proprietary software products. Design Systems Inc. has offices in New Jersey and markets its software products nationally. Mr. Dowd has a computer operations, systems, programming, and management background. His marketing and management expertise has helped shape a successful computer software company known for the quality of its products and for its ability to respond quickly to market demands.

Q1. Mr. Doud, what is the nature of your company's business?

A1. Computer consulting is our primary business. We provide custom programming as well as packages to our clients. In most cases, we provide customization, which is the modification of our packages to satisfy specific needs of our clients.

Q2. What is your target market in terms of types of businesses as well as types of computer equipment for which you provide software?

A2. Our market is broken down into segments, with the primary emphasis on distributors, chemical manufacturers, and processors, leasing organizations, and credit unions. These are our prime markets, but we also provide services to other manufacturing and service oriented firms. We primarily provide service to IBM customers for the System/36 and System/38. In addition to providing industry with specific consulting services, we market our System/36 security product.

Q3.   In the market's concern, what has a higher priority performance or security--and why?

A3.   Performance has the highest priority at the present time,with security seldom if ever mentioned by the client. The principal reason for this is that most top management is geared to look for and select the best performance. This is natural, because as security of information is not stressed, it is often overlooked. In addition, most top managers don't believe that they have a security problem and, accordingly, do not recognize the benefits of security.

Q4.   What are the major security concerns of companies in your market?

A4.   Unauthorized access to proprietary data is the major security concern of our clients. In addition to controlling access for theft, our clients are concerned about sabotage by disgruntled employees, and accidental damage by the curious.

Q5.   Do you sell products designed specifically to prevent unauthorized use or access to proprietary data? What level of market response have you received? If there is no overwhelming surge to acquire such products, why is this so? What would be required to convince your market to place a higher priority on security oriented products?

A5. Our product (Design Security) is designed to restrict access to those authorized by management to see proprietary data. The market response to date has been lukewarm. We are not selling sufficient numbers to classify the product as a success. In my opinion, there is a reluctance to acquire security oriented products for two reasons: (1) The user does not perceive a need for the product; does not believe that anyone in the organization would cause a problem; (2) users don't think their proprietary data is all that valuable or vulnerable. As for convincing people to protect their assets, it is difficult to say what is needed for this. Maybe it takes something to happen to someone close--almost like a burglary, which causes everyone in the neighborhood to go out and get a burglar alarm.

Q6. Are the software products you market known as "add-on"? Will you define that concept, please?

A6. Yes, our security package is considered an add-on--that is, a software product that, when added to your system, works with all the other software you have. System suppliers usually provide products you term add-ons.

Q7. Would the type of security support provided by your software be less expensive, more compatible and easier to use if it were already designed into the hardware product?

A7. It is difficult to say what the cost would be, because, for the most part, something like this would be built into the operating system. I think that compatibility can be provided by both the hardware vendor and the add-on manufacturer, but it will certainly be easier to implement if it comes with the operating system.

Q8. Do you foresee hardware vendors making a greater effort to design security support into their products in the future? What barriers have slowed such effort?

A8. Hardware vendors have made some effort to build security into their new operating systems. The major problem faced by most hardware vendors is compatibility of operating systems. Vendors are almost forced to wait until they introduce a completely new computer with a new operating system; otherwise they risk the possibility of sending out a new version that will be incompatible with the users' existing systems.

Q9. Do you believe it is a fair assumption that users of high tech products have the sole obligation for providing all their security support needs?

A9. I don't think there is much doubt about it. It is almost like a builder automatically providing a security system in every house he builds. I don't feel that the hardware vendors are under any obligation to provide a security system, although I believe that they may, some day, provide it as an extra option.

Q10. What internal security requirements do you use to minimize abuse of technology or theft of trade secrets by employees? Do you find those restraints effective, or would you like additional federal or state laws? If so, will you describe such laws?

A10. We use our security system to restrict information to employees who have the need to know. The restraints we have in place are probably adequate. I don't believe that adding federal and state laws will eliminate the security problem. Enforcement, and the related costs to the company, are a more difficult problem. Theft may be going on right now--but proving it in court can be extremely costly. The best theft preventive measure is to lock up the information so that it does not provide temptation.

Preventing Transfer of Technology
To Hostile Powers

One of the most compelling problems facing the computer industry is the federal government's concern over the transfer of technology to hostile powers, in particular the Soviet Union and Eastern Block countries. This concern has manifested itself in regulations implementing the Export Administration Act, which governs the flow of technology exports. The Defense and Commerce Departments are both directly involved with decisions that affect not only whether certain technology can be exported, but whether the exporter should be subject to penalties for failing to properly research the credibility of the buyer. Vendors have expressed a fear that review by Defense and Commerce will cause delays and impose restrictions that could impede the ability of domestic industry to compete in international markets.

For understanding of this problem and what it means to both the individual and our society, this author discussed the matter with leading expert in transfer technology: Mr. Michael A. Daniels, Esq., President of International Public Policy Research Corporation, located in Falls Church, Virginia. He said "The most significant issues raised by the problem of controlling the transfer of technology are twofold: first is the issue of diversion, theft, etc., of U.S. technology for military purposes by the Soviets and their allies; second is the issue of diversion, by friends and foes for competitive purposes. The federal govenment has a primary responsiblity for the national defense. If our high technology is stolen and used by enemies, they do not have to expend the billions we did for development. In addition, if we lose our technological lead, we will fall behind in internationl competition (affecting economic growth and costing jobs)."

As Mr. Daniels pointed out, the conflict between private industry and government is dollars vs. defense. In deep background briefings with senior government officials at both the Defense and State Departments, the following concerns were expressed:

(1) The West, in particular the U.S., remains an R&D center for Soviet technological development. The failure of the Soviet economy to produce high quality technical products demanded by its military has caused it to focus resources on acquiring such technology from the West. Intelligence reports indicate that military related technology acquired by Soviet intelligence services saved the Soviet military industry hundreds of millions of rubles, permitting them to conserve badly needed resources. In addition to preservation of resources, the acquisition of such technology enabled the Soviets to quickly gain a capability for increased military options against the West which would otherwise have taken additional years for development.

(2) The impact of Soviet efforts on our society has been to:

(a) Increase the individual taxpayer's burden by forcing him to pay for heavier than expected defense costs in order to maintain the West's technological advantage. As was pointed out by the State and Defense Department officials, the Soviets have a quantitative advantage. If they could also achieve a qualitative edge, the West could be vulnerable. This means that each instance of transfer to the Soviets causes an expenditure of U.S. money in new defense related technology to make up for the reduced qualitative edge. In effect, it is a never-ending pattern of pouring millions of tax dollars into catch-up, resulting in an ever-increasing individual tax burden. (b) Compel greater government market intervention than expected in order to identify and avoid loss of military oriented technology. On the international front, the U.S. has taken the lead among its allies to provide a consistant classification of militarily sensitive (dual use) technology which all have agreed to protect. In cooperation with its allies, the U.S. is also working to seize such technology in the stream of commerce to prevent delivery to the Soviets. Recent examples of such seizures in West Germany, Great Britain, Sweden and Japan attest to the effectiveness of such efforts. On the domestic front the regulations issued by the Departments of Commerce and Defense impose a burden on the exporter to determine the credibility of the buyer.

How serious is the exporter's duty to investigate the buyer's credentials? In interviews with senior Defense Department officials, they compared such duty to that of a fiduciary. The reasoning was that the right to export is granted by law; it is not inalienable. There is an underlying assumption of reliance by the government on the exporter's good faith. Failure to live up to the good faith expectation is a breach of trust, and exposes the exporter to such penalities (prison and fine) as provided by law. Illustrative would be the vendor of dual use (military/civilian capacity) technology (high speed computers, laser operated range finders, etc.) who receives an order from a Swedish company to buys its products. The buyer provides all necessary information required by the Export Administration Act regulations. Does the vendor still have a duty to further investigate the information provided by the buyer? According to the senior Defense Department officials with whom I discussed this hypothetical problem, the answer would depend on the particular facts. If the buyer's address was a post office box, or the buyer had no previous business history, the answer might be "yes." Those officials stressed that such matters would be reviewed on a case-by-case basis. The bottom line is seller beware! There is a clear duty to "go forward" and ask questions. The spirit of the fiduciary obligation imposed on vendors requires them to be an active participant in preventing dual use (military/civilian) technology from being transferred to the Soviet block.

Clearly, the problem of identifying and preventing the transfer of dual use technology to the Soviets will occupy a considerable amount of time, effort and resources, in addition to involving the federal government in day-to-day marketing decisions by exporters of high technology products. It is that constituancy that has raised the most criticism of the federal government's efforts to control the transfer of technology. The contention (touched upon by Mr. Daniels) has been that (a) any interference in market decisions will be detrimental to their ability to compete internationally with Europe or Japan, since those countries will sell to the Soviets what the Soviets cannot buy here; and (b) if the Soviets want a certain type of technology they will acquire it through espionage activities that are being conducted almost openly in the Silicon Valley. For those reasons, the exporters argue that the program to control the transfer of technology is a waste of taxpayer dollars and also costs jobs and economic growth by reducing the American's competitive advantage.

Where does the truth lie? The senior State and Defense Department officials rebutted the exporters' argument by showing that Japan and our European allies were indeed coordinating efforts to control the transfer of technology, so that failure to purchase technology in the U.S. will not lead to sales of that same technology by a competitor. At the same time, those officials took pains to point out that the process of identifying dual use technology is market sensitive, with U.S. bowing to market pressures in permitting the transfer of certain types of "low technology" products. So, like virtually all other issues surrounding the new technology, this one has its own variant of gray.

It is important for the individual to understand that this issue will continue to affect the pocketbook in terms of tax dollars invested in defense-related technology to keep ahead of the Soviets and in jobs lost to competitors who divert proscribed technology.

NOTES

CHAPTER V

THE ART OF NEGOTIATING

Many people seem to perceive negotiation as angry, uncontrolled confrontation, initiated or complicated by lawyers who are paid by the hour and couldn't care less about the problem concerned. Unfortunately, such perceptions tend to be accurate because most people, be they lawyers or business executives, don't fully understand how to control the negotiating process sufficiently to avoid the damage, disruption, and polarization of needless rancor.

A. THE NATURE OF NEGOTIATION

Perception over substance, that grand illusion, has often been viewed as the key to effective negotiations. Like most simplistic solutions, it is only half right. Negotiation is a process that weaves a web of interrelationships designed to solve a particular problem. It involves trust, time, circumstances, information and egos. The objective is limited. A contract for acquiring a computer system is specific enough to provide a basis for negotiation. A general agreement to stop all war, such as the Kellogg-Briand Pact is so universal as to be useless. The needs of both parties to an understanding should be determined by specific objectives. For instance, performance, support, recourse and payment are legitimate needs, not the feelings about a company's personnel policy or its definition of charitable organiztions. The process of negotiation creates an interpersonal relationship between parties, to achieve a limited goal.

B. THE PROCESS: WHY AND HOW IT WORKS

Time, circumstance and information are the keys.

Time: Both parties to an agreement need sufficient time to determine particular needs, establish priorities, and organize resources. For this reason, preparation is essential. Know who you are, what you want, when you need it, and what you're going to trade to get it (money or product). There is a classic case of an insurance company executive who saw a software product demonstrated at a trade show. Impressed, he asked the vendor for a contract and signed on the spot, committing his company to an immediate payout of $75,000 without any assurance of performance. Worse, the trade secret limitations in the vendor's contract restricted use and access to the product to such an extent that the insurance company could not integrate the software into its business operations. When the vendor was subsequently asked by the company to make changes in the already signed contract, it said "tough, but that's your problem." The insurance company executive had failed to give his company time to review and understand the obligation it was assuming. Result, sandbagged!

No negotiations occured, because the deal was cast in concrete before the buyer had time to understand its own needs. In business deals, patience is more than a virtue; it is a key element in formulating the preparation needed to define expectations.

The "Bum's Rush" is a ploy commonly used by vendors to expedite the user's decision-making process through incentives such as reduction in cost, or guaranteeing a delivery window. The objective is to create tremendous pressure compelling the user to make an immediate decision. The vendor's scenario is the buyer taking its time to understand business needs, compare alternatives, and formulate options--in essence, preparation! If the vendor can force a decision before the user determines its own needs, then the vendor has controlled the negotiations. By using pressure ploys, vendors attempt to shortcut the user's time requirements, creating an imminent need where none may actually exist. Like sleight of hand, "now you see it and now you don't." So the need for the product becomes a question of immediate dollars, instead of long-term benefit.

Time is money! The more time spent understanding and preparing, the less money wasted. Pressure ploys can be resisted by common sense and a perception that a long term view spells satisfaction of needs compared with artificially generated short-term incentives.

<u>Circumstance</u>:   Closely allied with time is the context confronting each party. This is the circumstance that determines leverage.   For example, if the vendor has just started in business, it needs to create and control a market quickly, or if a buyer finds that a particular product can perform a crucial application, then it needs to acquire that product quickly. Those are "immediate" needs that reduce leverage, making it difficult for any such party to compel formulation of a favorable agreement.   Weak circumstances do not usually result in a "balanced" agreement, no matter how effective the negotiator.

There are, however, tactics that the weakest party can use to mask its problems. The most common is to create a facade that, it is hoped, will not be scrutinized closely. Take the small software company that had an opportunity to sell an application software product to its first major client. The president of that software company acted very "laid-back" during his initial contact with the client. Follow-up contact was friendly but casual, mostly with the client's technicians, who were excited about the product. During one phone conversation the president of that software company "let slip" that his product's price will probably be raised within the following week. Within one day, he received a phone call from the client's vice president of technical services imploring permission to sign the vendor's contract before the price rise became effective. The software company's president acted "shocked" that the client knew of the impending price change and reluctantly agreed, after some "arm-twisting," to hold the price at its current level if the contract was signed within 24 hours. The truth of the matter was that the software company had virtually no other clients, was about to "go under," and desperately needed the client's business. By "playing poker," the president of that software company bluffed a larger, more powerful organization into signing a contract that did not even provide a promise that the software would function in accordance with its specifications.

This scenario was not due so much to the nerve of the software company's president (which helped), but was more a result of the client's ineptitude, which is unfortunately typical of most large (bureaucratic) organizations.

The lesson is: illusion over substance! Project your own reality. If you look confident and act confident, people will believe you are confident. Human nature likes to accommodate. No one wants "a hassle." If it is made easy enough, most people will follow the behavior pattern laid down by someone in whom they have confidence. Translation: trust! So, even if the circumstance is weak, by disclosing only information that supports the reality you want to project, an illusion will be created masking actual fact. Result: the party with the most believable projection will generally control the negotiations.

Information: As stated above, perception is a product of information. Candor is wonderful, but its place in negotiations should be limited to creating a favorable perception. For instance, that same client who signed the software company's "as is" contract was initially "set-up" by its technicians who told the vendor how badly they needed that product. What incentive did that vendor have to change its contract position, or to be less than certain of its control? Answer: none! It had received information which said that the buyer was desperate and would give anything for that product; so, regardless of its actual circumstance, it was in a strong contract position.

Information limited to conveying a particular perception is the rule in negotiations. Don't blab, trickle! Tell the other side only what you what them to know about your perception of the situation. The software company president did just that in dealing with the client. He never indicated his desperate straits. Indeed, he projected a business-like professional calm that gave no hint of weakness. No one is suggesting false representations, but there is no compelling reason to disclose every fact. There is a chasm between misrepresentation and total candor--a chasm, galactic in size, permitting a negotiator to control the other person's perception by parcelling out limited amounts of information. For example, take the user who decided to acquire a multi-vendor system. One of its key requirements was to assure a smooth working relationship between the participating vendors so they could respond quickly and effectively to a system failure. By indicating that concern at the outset, it became a focal point. Tying its resolution to the selection of one of several competing vendor teams created a perception that the ultimate agreement was performance-oriented. Information was disclosed to each competing vendor team focusing on that issue. The fact that the user was so far down the line in the selection process that it couldn't withdraw, regardless of vendor response to that issue, was not disclosed. Indeed, a competitive environment was created to foster the user's projection of control. Meaning the vendors were led to believe that the user would walk. Clearly, if total candor was the rule, no vendor would exert itself to meet the user's requirement for bi-lateral cooperation. However, in this illustration, only specific information was disclosed, focused on the particular issue to avoid discussion of other matters such as the user's actual need. In effect, the information released molded the response.

So the formula for using time, circumstance, and information is:

a. Determine needs. Take the time to prepare, by formulating business expectations that the vendor must satisfy.

b. Communicate needs. Create the circumstance that the vendor ought to perceive. Project a perception that best supports business expectations.

c. Limit information to particular issues that support the desired projection. Focus on those issues to avoid diffusion that might undercut the desired illusion.

d. Use dialogue patiently to reinforce the issues in point, molding a response that best satisfies expectations.

In no event should there be disclosure of all internal problems, fears or worries. Indeed, the dialogue should be conducted in a businesslike manner, focusing on particular issues important to satisfaction of needs. The result will be control! The vendor is compelled to focus on the particular problems delineated by the user, instead of playing ambiguous games designed to mesh issues, confuse the situation, and expose a weakness that can be used as leverage.

The process of negotiation is a molding of perceptions. To work, it requires:

a. Trust. Even though representing an opposing interest, the negotiator should project fairness and probity; someone willing to listen with respect and understanding. No one wants to talk to a person they dislike. Building a relationship based on willingness to listen is the first step to communication. In line with that, is credibility. If the negotiator is known for deceit, then the vendor's representative will have no faith in assurances about fairness. The other side must be able to "rely" on the information received. If it cannot do that, there is no turst, and the negotiator becomes a liability.

    b. Identifying common grounds: Everyone wants to agree that the reason for even talking to each other is to resolve the transaction. This type of general common ground is the initial base for any further negotiations. From that point, the negotiator moves from the general to the specific. Starting with common agreement on broad issues, the dialogue then moves forward to the specifics of each issue, identifying what, when, where and how (the nuts and bolts). Points where there are conflict are circumvented and held aside until all matters of common agreement are identified. The negotiator then returns to those points, probing in detail to determine the reason for conflict. This process often continues for a significant period of time. Again, patience is a virtue. Talking for hours about conflicting issues may be the only way to find out what makes the other side so resolute about a problem. The manner of conversation is also important. Generally, it is relaxed, but sharp exchanges are often necessary to emphasize the seriousness of a situation, particularly if a party is suspected of "playing games" by not directly responding to issues, confusing matters with extraneous facts, and generally being evasive.

c. Resolving conflict by trade-off: Hyperbole is the essence of marketing, and so it is in negotiations. Both sides are selling by hyping their respective value. Each appeals to the other's self-interest, measuring value in terms of benefit instead of dollars. For instance, a vendor will try to convince an end-user that the value of its particular product should not be measured in the dollars charged for the benefit produced, resulting in an actual cost that is negligable when compared with the expected results (higher productivity and lower cost). The end-user will try to convince the vendor to change its contract position, by touting the ripple effect of other sales relationships. Both sides enhance their relative value by focusing not on the actual transaction but on its effect. As the adage goes, "sell the 'sizzle' not the steak," and both sides follow that prescription when describing their relative merits. It is within that context that the line between fact and expectation often blurs. The vendor sells its product as the "no problem solution" to the user's business needs. What the vendor really means is that the product should work in accordance with its functional specifications. The reality is that the vendor has not thoroughly studied the user's business, so it cannot know the particular business applications needed. Meanwhile, the buyer sells itself as a model for other prospects, a marketing tool that the vendor can use to attract other sales. The marketing tool tactic pre-supposes that the buyer's name exudes an influence that will significantly affect the market.

The end result of all the hyperbole, touting, and puffing is the trade-off of conflicting requirements to create a mutually satisfactory agreement. Such trade-off is cast in the context of "good faith" or "fairness" which pre-supposes the honorable intent of both parties. Each side agrees to modify its requirements on the basis of "sensitivity" to the other's needs.

So, molding means establishing a relationship of mutual trust and respect, identifying areas of collaborative interest, isolating conflicting requirements, and using hyperbole to assuage anxiety by focusing on sensitivity (good faith) to motivate change of positions. In a nutshell, that is the process of negotiation.

C. NEGOTIATION TYPES: WARM AND COLD

There are two major types of negotiating postures: collaborative, where both parties strive for a long relationship,

305

being sensitive to the other's needs; and competitive, where one's gain is the other's loss. Various aspects of both models or types are often intertwined so the actual negotiations are a combination of sensitivity and toughness (as with any human relationship).

Competitive: A classic example of this model, or type, is the ultimatum. It is used, in a limited manner, only if one side believes it has sufficient clout to compel the other to accept. To be effective, the ultimatum must come at the end of negotiations and only after the other side has invested significant time and effort in the process. For instance, a vendor is in the process of negotiating with an end user to acquire a computer system. Months have elapsed between the RFP and the Proposal. The vendor knows that the user needs the system, is getting tired of wrangling over "legal" interpretation, and would like to focus its energies on marketing rather than on contract problems. The vendor surmises that the user has invested too much time to start all over again, so acting on that conclusion, the vendor toughens its negotiating position, arguing that the end-user must accept the standard contract. Shocked by this turn-around, the end user is faced with a dilemma. Assurance that the product will perform has been eliminated by the vendor's sudden revision to its standard contract. If the user rejects the vendor's position, it will walk. Faced with the prospect of having to start the process all over again, the user will generally accept the vendor's ultimatum. This is a common situation that could have been avoided by maintaining competitive pressure--dealing with at least two vendors up until the last minute, to compel a responsive posture. In such a circumstance, neither of the two vendors would have had the leverage to compel execution of its standard contract, since the user had an option.

Delivery of an ultimatum is often done in a low-key, matter-of-fact manner. The most common context is the phrase "corporate policy." "We can't change this contract, because corporate policy won't permit every contract to be administered differently." Another variation, "I understand your position, but I'm bound by corporate policy, which stipulates that only the Board of Directors can make any changes." Both are effective vehicles for delivering the "take it or leave it" ultimatum.

Competitive contracts generally take a short view of relationships. They are extreme positions, most advantageous to the issuing party and detrimental to the recipient. The issuing party shows little if any flexibility, pressuring the other party with hyperbole and blandishments ("we really ignore the contract"), but being totally unwilling to make any written changes. For example, if one were to buy a micro-computer from a major vendor (and insisted on changes to that vendor's standard written contract), other than receiving assurances that several thousand other users have had no problems (a totally unsubstantiated blandishment) the user would be unsuccessful. It would have the option of signing the standard contract or not buying the micro-computer. There would be no contract change.

Faced with a competitive contract, the other side is often left with the following choices:

a. Walk--drop the effort and deal with another party. This is often difficult, but it is realistic if performance is not going to be supported by the contract. The cost of starting all over again is never as high as the cost of a lemon and of the vendor's non-support.

b. Sign--a truly desperate act, requiring enormous soul-searching. Any organization sandbagged into such circumstance should consider bagging its management.

c. Negotiate--attempt to turn a competitive relationship into a collaborative one. This is an enormously frustrating and often unsuccessful task. The other side probably would not have taken its extreme position if it didn't believe it had the clout to deliver. Every now and then, however, the underdog perserveres. With patience, persistance, and whatever competitive pressure that can be created, the competitive party is sometimes turned into a collaborator. Take the largest and most powerful computer vendor in the country, which was trying to sell a $3.5 million dollar computer system to a bank. The vendor handed down its standard, unvarying, onerous contract. The bank's outside counsel blanched, attempted to argue with the vendor and was told that the contract was "policy." Realizing its situation, the bank's management authorized its counsel to "keep talking" to that vendor while it searched for alternatives. The bank's attorney then projected a competitive environment, indicating that the vendor's contract position was unacceptable and that other vendors were being contacted. In fact, the bank did seek other vendors, finding one that offered a comparable product and who was willing to be responsive. The original computer vendor suddenly became less dogmatic about its contractual terms, making (believe it or not) modifications to its previously sacrosanct agreement. Ultimately, that vendor did sign that bank, but not before it completely reversed its position, making contractual changes that met the bank's business expectations. The bank's dogged persistance, coupled with the competitive pressure created by its attorneys, had paid off.

So the situation is not always hopeless. When confronted by a competitive situation, there are options, one of which is to buckle down, be persistant, and turn the situation into a collaborative relationship.

<u>Collaborative</u>: This is the generic description for the most common form of negotiation, where each side is willing to modify positions to accommodate the other's needs. This is particularly true when there is a competitive environment and anxiety exists about which vendor will be selected. Confronting such circumstances motivates sensitivity. Illustrative is the governmental agency that delayed choosing one of two vendors until all of its contractual requirements had been accepted by the primary candidate. Using the alternate candidate as the "strawman" the government agency compelled the primary candidate to literally restructure its contract position. Such a turn about was accomplished by the negotiator who slowly, using trust, sensitivity and understanding, conveyed "insights" to that vendor allowing it to draw the conclusion that its integration of those "insights" in the contract was critical to the agency's selection decision. By trading off minor requirements,

showing a sensitivity towards the vendor's needs, the negotiator was able to establish a long term mutually reciprocal agreement satisfactory to both parties.

Most collaborative negotiations contain similar characteristics: a desire by both parties for a long term relationship, a willingness to accomodate the other's needs and a low-key dialogue directed at solving the problem instead of salving ego. Based on mutual trust supported by a contract that assures performance through recourse, a collaborative relationship is the model for most constructive business agreements.

Approach:

Preparation is the key to tactics. There is no substitute for good old-fashioned work. The more thorough the preparation, the easier the negotiation. There are two aspects of preparation; one is gathering the information and the other is the team approach.

Gathering Information: This is critical if a party is to understand its business objectives. No matter how good the negotiator, it is the client that provides the ammunition. So the questions of what, when, where and how determine the business applications that must be automated, the resources needed to support automation, and the time period and method of payment. In addition, the negotiating parties must establish priorities that are critical to an agreement-- priorities such as assurance of performance, and training and maintenance support, as well as recourse in the event of failure. The actual details for incorporating those priorities will depend on the negotiator's ability to motivate vendor accommodation. To put it succinctly: if you don't know what you want, stay home and save your breath!

Information about the other side generates power. As in a previous example, where a vendor knew that the end-user was desperate for the product, an ultimatum was the result of that inside information. So, in any situation where one side finds another's weakness, an opening is created for imposition instead of accommodation. For that reason, the phrase "playing it close to the vest" has real significance. Too often, inexperienced technicians or managers willingly "blab" all their problems to the "friendly and sympathetic" sales representative. By the time actual contract negotiations begin, the vendor knows the user's weaknesses and can exploit them to compel a favorable decision. It is important that during the informal probing, which occurs after initial contacts, any information released relates solely to the application point and does not go beyond that criteria to include the user's imminent business problems.

Otherwise, product need becomes a weakness that vendors can leverage to compel favorable decision. One of the difficult problems confronting managers is keeping to the facts: telling only what is necessary to describe application needs, and adding no extraneous information about market requirements, pressure from upper management, or the importance of a successful project to career advancement. As they say in the detective stories, "anything you say will be used against you." So it is with negotiations, which are exploitative in nature. Each side probes and pushes to find a weakness (hot button) it can use to extract concessions or favorable decision. Being "close" with the facts is critical to avoiding loss of control which makes the difference between negotiating a favorable contract and being compelled to sign an onerous agreement.

The Team Approach: Who talks to the vendor, as much as what is said can shape negotiations. After initital contacts, all information should be channeled through the manager, up through the time that the two main candidates have been selected. In no event should technicians, except for skilled consultants, deal directly with the vendor. Such individuals have too narrow a focus for the broad business issues that constitute most commercial transactions. In addition to having tunnel vision, they are often naive, believing that the vendor will act beyond contract limitations to meet user business requirements. For that reason, discipline is an essential ingredient in controlling information released to vendors. The manager should establish procedures and guidelines limiting contact between technician and vendor sales representatives, to avoid being sandbagged by overeager and naive technicians.

The attorney should be involved from the beginning--helping to shape the legal structure expressed in the RFP as business expectations. One often hears of the dichotomy between legal and business needs. Anyone believing in that fairytale should stick to <u>Alice</u> <u>in</u> <u>Wonderland</u>. Every business expectation--such as performance, training and maintenance--has its counterpart in the legal structure needed to assure that such expectations will be satisfied. They are sides of the same coin. Treating them differently, as exclusive unrelated concepts, is tantamount to erecting a building without a skeletal structure.

After the selection process has narrowed the choice to at least two vendors, it is the attorney who should take control of the negotiations, molding the vendors, as previously indicated, to select the one most responsive. One of the key problems confronting users is choosing the right attorney. There is a fiction that all lawyers are alike, meaning every lawyer can handle any legal problem.

Unfortunately, many business executives subscribe to that myth, leaving themselves exposed to naive or unprincipled attorneys who know nothing about high technology agreements. Witness the multi-million dollar real estate organization that had its general counsel negotiate the acquisition of a multi-vendor computer system costing about $250,000. Clearly, real estate law did not prepare that general counsel to understand the type of contractual assurances his client would need to support its business expectations. The result was that there was a great paragraph in the contract on indemnification but nothing on assurances for performance, support and training. You guessed it! The system failed to work, the contract offered no recourse, and the user was stuck with its thumb in the wrong place, spending even more money to fix something that should have worked in the first place! An attorney, like a consultant, should know the industry, and how to realistically assure that the contract will support performance. Choose counsel carefully, look at credentials, and be prepared to pay for the best.

An experienced attorney should be able to mold the competing parties to a position most favorable to the client. With preparation, information gathered and released (supporting client perception), as well as teamwork between manager and attorney, the negotiator should be able to exploit vendor concerns thereby creating an agreement that meets business needs.

D.   The Final Stage:

Two stages constitute the negotiating process. The informal probing stage discussed above occurs when neither side is, theoretically, discussing a contract but is, instead, discussing mutual business expectations. Then there is the final stage, where the written contract becomes the focus of discussion. During this stage, ploys are sometimes used to induce anxiety, control issues, and generally dominate the relationship. Such ploys would be:

a.   Good-guy/bad guy: An overused but generally effective tactic. It continues throughout the entire negotiating relationship. Its objective is to compel the other side to be more responsive to the "good-guy" half of the partnership. By using the old principle of "honey and vinegar," the other side is expected to gravitate to the warmer half who although stressing the dominance of the "bad guy," is sincerely interested in the "working out" of issues to avoid antagonizing the ogre. Played right, this can be an effective tool to motivate the vendor to change its position. The good guy is almost always the manager or consultant, while the attorney plays the heavy, although the roles can be switched, depending on issues and circumstance.

A simple example of how this ploy functions can be illustrated by a husband-and-wife house-hunting expedition. The young couple meet the ebullient real estate agent bubbling with fantasies on which they can spend their money. The husband (bad guy) is quiet; the wife (good guy) is responsive but deferential to the husband's opinion (final judgement). The real estate agent drives them to a typical ranch home designed for mediocrity and rapid obsolescence, effervescing fantasies of castles, cookies and carry-out Chinese food. The wife nods appreciably throughout the agent's monologue, adding expressions of agreement. The husband assumes a stoic posture with not even a glimmer of a smile. Every now and then, he whispers a clearly deprecating remark to his wife about the condition of the walls, floors, etc. At the end of the house tour, the husband and wife confer and the good guy half advises the real estate agent that her husband is not terribly impressed. Trying to make the sale the agent responds with questions. The husband states that the house is not worth the investment involved, and indicates that he doesn't have time to go into the matter with any great detail. The wife gives the agent their home phone number and advises him to call if there is a change in price. The next day, the agent calls and lowers the price in a negotiating session.

In simplistic terms, that is how good guy/bad guy should

work: motivating the other side to change its position to appease, or avoid antagonizing, the heavy. Translating that to a business situation, there are various versions that can be played--but all require consistency. In one scenario, both sides to a computer transaction met at the customer's place of business. The user's manager and attorney, the vendor's sales representative and counsel were present. Bursting suddenly in the room, the user's senior vice president glared at the vendor team and raged that all vendors are crooks--out to use legal gobblygook to mask their lack of performance. Had the manager not been there, the vice president would have thrown the vendor team out. Turning, he left, closing the door with a bang. There was a moment of silence and the vendors representative, shaken by the sudden appearance, rage, and disappearance of the senior vice president, stated that the vendor would dog all that was necessary to make that individual happy. The ploy had worked! The vendor had been motivated to accommodate the user's business needs.

Two players can also use a version of this ploy. The attorney, taking an "I'm from Missouri" attitude, approaches the vendor with blatant skepticism. The manager, offering the vendor a warmer attitude, makes it clear that in the end it is the lawyer that has to be satisfied (parallel with house-hunting vignette). In most instances, the attorney does little or no raging. He is quiet, reserved but emphatic, saving indignation for those situations where the vendor balks. At that point, there is usually a discussion between the vendor and the manager, where the latter asks for help to find a way of resolving the situation (appeasing the attorney). The anxiety induced by the attorney's distrust can be used as a motivator to compel accommodation by the vendor.

In situations where there is an outside consultant, variations on that theme can be even more diverse. The attorney can be the good guy in situations involving detailing of technical requirements (the consultant has to be happy with assurance of interface compatibility), and the bad guy involving language accommodation demands (if it is not in writing the attorney won't go for it!). Such a ploy is often effective in dealing with multi-vendor situations where the objective is to combine the vendors into a smooth working relationship to meet the user's requirements. The attorney and consultant work to split the hardware and software vendors, creating the appearance that the weaker entity (usually the software vendor) is a liability to the former because there is no assurance that it can perform or fully interface its customized software with packaged (off-the-shelf) software products. The objective is to pressure the hardware vendor into assuming the obligations of assuring a

319

smooth working relationship between itself and the software provider. The threat that a deal will be lost because of another party often stimulates the appropriate response.

So good guy/bad guy, with its bogeyman variations, is effective because it induces fear that the deal will be lost unless a certain party is placated. The informal mediation used by the good guy to mold the vendor is key to the effectiveness of that ploy. The downside is that just "play acting" fools no one. The parties must be sincere and consistent, and must appear to be honest and reasonable, or the strategy will backfire and the user will lose credibility.

b. What if: This hypothetical question is used to clarify ambiguous phrases, pinning down the other side to specific details. For instance, assume a maintenance issue of cure. How soon will the vendor respond and cure a failure? Generally, the answer is best efforts. The next step is to pose "what if" queries to define the area of best efforts, pinning down specifics. For example, the negotiator would follow-up with such questions as what would be the average cure time, what if the defect cannot be cured within that time frame, what alternatives are available, etc. By constantly pressing the issue with hypothetical questions, the vendor becomes more involved with details and is drawn away from the generalized response of best efforts. Key to the "what if" tactic is persistence; constantly pressing the same issue, pinning down details to compel disclosure.

c. Fight and trade: Closely allied with "what if" is the tactic used to resolve conflict after disclosure. Illustrative is that same maintenance situation. The "what if" tactic has compelled disclosure that the vendor can generally cure system problems within four (4) hours but refuses to make a commitment beyond best efforts. The issue is resolution of conflicting positions. The user is demanding liquidated damages for failure to so cure within that four hour period; the vendor is refusing. In addition, the user also requires that the vendor pay for another party to cure the system failure if the inability to cure extends beyond one business day; again the vendor refuses. Discussion continues on those points, with the user insisting that unless it receives assurances of a safety net, the contract is at break point. The vendor indicates it doesn't want to pay-out liquidated damages and it is not happy about a third party taking over its business. Counsel for the user suggests a trade: demands for liquidated damages and one-day activation of third party assistance are dropped; in return, the vendor guarantees 100% data load contingency arrangements and agrees to third party intervention if the problem cannot be resolved within thirty (30) days. The parties find a common ground. Extreme user positions are modified to provide a safety net (contingency arrangement) while the vendor is not threatened by liquidated damages if it fails to cure within a relatively short period of time. Third party intervention is pushed off far enough time to provide the vendor a fair opportunity to cure. Result: the parties can feel comfortable with an arrangement that satisfies common needs.

    d.   Sincerity and reason: Throughout the negotiations, a low key, reasonable and sincere approach should prevail. Disarming the other side with sincerity and a reasonable sensitivity to needs goes a long way toward minimizing conflict. Such an approach fosters the perception that everyone is acting in good faith and desires only to create a fair agreement. No one likes someone to shout at them, belittle their expertise, or denigrate their character. Scorn breeds indignation and rage polarizes, disrupting communication. To maintain an open dialogue, the parties have to reciprocate each other's good faith. Human nature generally accommodates the most comfortable behavior pattern. So if an approach of reason and sincerity is used to discuss a problem (conflict in position) the other side will often reciprocate. In this way, even the most probing questions can be asked, or extreme positions discussed, without disrupting communication between the parties. An additional benefit is that a business relationship developed within such an approach tends to be less prone to distrust and more flexible in resolving post contract administration problems. People who feel comfortable with each other can work well together.

e. Pyrotechnics: The age-old scenario of negotiations. A cigar chomping, bug-eyed, red-faced, fuming antagonist looms over the other side, his face inches away exuding scorn. A rare occurrence, but rage and indigation, if applied to the right situation in a limited dosage, can induce sufficient anxiety to motivate a change in position. For example, take a situation where both parties have used a seasoned approach but the discussion has bogged down in conflict. The user's attorney has been quietly repeating his client's need for assurance of system performance and the other side has indicated that such performance will occur, but refuses to permit system testing prior to acceptance. The user and its attorney had previously agreed that assurance of system performance was a breakpoint issue. After the vendor has refused for the eighth time, counsel for the user suddenly explodes. He declares that the other side is acting in bad faith. He begins a tirade that includes table-pounding, finger-pointing and angry indignation. The other side is caught off-guard with the surprise burst of outrage. They deny bad faith, causing the user's attorney to grow even angrier. The sudden explosion of rage and indignation has made performance-testing the key issue. The deal is at breakpoint, and the other side has to decide immediately if their investment of time, effort, and resources is to collapse over this one issue. The monkey is on their back, and they won't be free until they either relent or reject the user's requirement. Pyrotechnics has compelled a decision crucial to the deal.

Effective use of pyrotechnics requires: (1) knowing which issues are crucial; and (2) the sudden and apparently genuine use for specific issues within the context of a reasonable approach. The effect is surprise, which expedites decision. However, like its label, this type of behavior can be explosive. Unless used by an expert, the situation can blow-up, shutting off negotiations, threatening the initiator with a loss of credibility. Rage can be believed only if it is used sparingly.

The antidote for pyrotechnics is calm, quiet low key posture. There is nothing more devastating then confronting anger with an unruffled calm. In the above situation, the vendor's attorney should have replied calmly, soothingly, and without hesitation to the outburst directed by the other side. A controlled, businesslike, low-key response is like a blanket over a flame, snuffing out the fire of indignation with reasoned consistency.

f. Walk-out: Related to pyrotechnics is the walk-out, which can be either an adjournment (clear the air) or a shut-down (don't call me, I'll call you). The walk-out is used as an adjunct to pyrotechnics. If after expressing rage and indignation there is still no change of position by the other side, then initiator has two choices: give up or walk out. If the issue has been cleared with the client as a breakpoint, then the initiator is in a powerful position. He can call an adjournment and have the parties pair off, with the two negotiators and decision-makers holding separate discussion. Thereafter, if the discussions still indicate lack of progress, he can terminate and walk out, leaving the other side with the burden of having caused the shut-off. However, even in that situation there should be an under-current of reasonableness. The initiator should indicate a willingness to listen to informal discussions. If anxiety motivates the other side, then discussions will resume with either party losing face. If the initiator attempts to revive discussions, the loss of credibility will be devastating. His client may as well sign the other side's contract and forget about meaningful negotiations.

g. Sandbag vs Salami: The difference between the sales representative of the vendor and its decision-maker, is authority. The former cannot bind, the latter can. For that reason, actual contract negotiations should involve only the decision-maker. However, the molding process underlying effective negotiations makes the sales representative a prime player. Before any actual sit-down discussion occurs, the competitive climate is created to pressure the sales representative into assurances that would be binding on its principal. Wait a minute! How can the sales representative bind its principal if it has no authority? Answer, by the user extracting written concessions during the selection process, incorporating them into a contract, and making agreement a prime determinant for selection. In effect, the selection process will not be completed until the vendor agrees to the assurances provided by its sales representative. It is called sandbag! As the competition becomes more intense, the sales representative is pressured by the user to be more responsive. Only written assurances will be accepted, with a clear understanding that they will be included in the contract. By the time the decision-maker is aware of the transaction, his sales representative (to protect its commission), has, in effect, accepted an agreement responsive to the user. Failure of the decision-maker to execute that document would mean a loss of face as well as of the deal. The sales representative, to protect his commission and the new client relatonship, pressures the decision-maker to accede.

Such a circumstance is different from the usual scenario where the sales representative and the user "hammer out" a contract. The sales representative then takes that document back to its corporate office for approval. Result: disaster! The user is trapped in a morass of time-consuming frustraton. First there's a long wait. Time becomes precious, with pressure building on the end-user to consummate the deal. Then the sales representative responds, terribly apologetic about the delay and hopeful (positively ebullient) that all problems have been solved. There is one little glitch, however. His management objects to a particular section in the agreement, and unless this problem is resolved the deal may be in jeopardy. The provision has to do with performance assurance. "Corporate" wants payment on delivery and will cover performance through the warranty of repair or replace. Four months ago the user thought all had been settled, with performance testing as a condition for payment. The sales representative agrees with the user, is apologetic, but cannot do much about "home office policy" (note ultimatium).

The vendor is betting that the user's investment of time and resources in protracted negotiations has limited its options, preventing recourse to an alternative vendor (since that would require an additional investment of time and money). Generally, the vendor is right! In the above example, the outcome would be an agreement by the user to "lop off" that provision in its contract. The sales representative assures the user that all problems have been solved, and there is another wait as the contract is again sent to "corporate" for approval. Finally, the sales representative responds and management now finds another problem, this time maintenance support. It refuses to lock itself into any turn-around cure period. So it goes. The tactic is known as "salami." Each point that the end user thought it had won months ago is sliced away, one by one, until it is essentially executing the vendor's standard contract. The remedy: don't rely on contractual agreements worked out with sales representatives <u>before</u> removing competitive pressure. At the point where the agreement is ready for submission, advise the sales representative that the nearest competitor will also receive a copy, with the rule being first in time is first in right. In other words, make it a horserace. This will create enormous competitive pressure and blunt any attempt to use the salami ploy.

Remember, authority is double-edged. Once sucked in by the sales representative's assurances, the user is trapped, losing all leverage and ending up bound by the vendor's standard terms and conditions. By maintaining competitive pressure you compel the vendor to deliver on those assurances or lose the deal.

h.   Home Turf: A key tactic in negotiations is comfort. Psychologists have indicated that a new environment causes disorientation, creating anxiety and disrupting concentration.   So always try to hold the actual negotiating session at your place of business.   For example, knowing the restroom's location is an added comfort, reducing unnecessary tension.   Remember that negotiating takes concentration and an enormous amount of effort, no matter how easy it looks. So a little familiarization goes a long way.

The tactics discussed all work together to create a process that results in a satisfactory transaction.   Managing that process requires teamwork, effort, flexibility, and patience. our instant-gratification-society often fails to appreciate the complexity of that process and the expertise required to make it work.   This is apparent in the best of business organizations. Psychological warfare aside, many people expect the "gun" to instantly make the other side accept its terms.   Such expectation is often fostered by the "guns" hired at outrageous fees to negotiate contracts.   As indicated in this Chapter, the reality is, of course, totally different.   Hard work, effort, thought, skill, information, time, patience, and support are all required to make it work.   As with any investment--there is a cost.   The weakest-link syndrome affects the final result.   For instance, if the client is short-sighted then no matter how good the negotiator, all efforts will be doomed.

So, before entering the process, both the client and negotiator should take a long-term view, analyze the effort and its cost, and calculate the bottom-line! Knowing when to pack-it-in is as important as knowing when to go for it!

CHAPTER VI

THE FUTURE OUTLOOK

A. WHAT DOES IT ALL MEAN

Throughout this Book, discussion was centered on acquiring and protecting software technology. Since it is clear that nearly everyone is affected by computer technology, whether at home or in business, an urgent need exists to understand its changing nature and the perils it poses. In much the same way that the lives of agricultural workers in England were affected by the Industrial Revolution, ours are shaped by technology in terms of emerging job opporunities, businesses, education facilities and procedures, family relationships, etc., the only difference being that instead of the process taking a hundred years, it has been telescoped to twenty--with no end in sight. The pressures created by the dynamics and constant, rapid changes in all aspects of a society can devastate social institutions, unhooking the moral linchpins such as family, personal integrity and respect for authority. So the real questions addressed in this chapter is not the futuristic "Star Wars" wizardry that has descended on our hapless selves, but how to successfully cope with the pressures generated by the dynamics of such technology.

B.   THE TRENDS

The leading futurist of our time is, clearly, John Naisbett. In his book Megatrends, he identifies ten overall trends (Megatrends) generated by the new technology which will affect our lives.   An examination of those concepts would be helpful to answering the question of how to succeed in coping with and using the technology.

1.   The first trend is the transformation of our economy from an industrial to an informational (service oriented) base. Instead of relying on depleting natural resources like fossil fuel, the merging of technologies (such as computers, lasers, telephone and television) has created an integrated communications network.   The energy that moves business is the information generated and communicated by that integrated network.   In effect, we now mass-produce knowledge the way we mass-produce cars.   The more information, the greater the impact and the more successful the effort.   Therefore, information is power.

What does this mean to a business or society?   Basically, our most valuable resource is information.   As we discussed in the section of this book that dealt with privacy, most people still don't seem to realize the value of accumulated information.   For that reason, the evolution of giant data banks has been a quiet, almost unheralded event, generating little or no public inquiry as to who owns the information contained in those electronic files, what can be done with that information, and who can access it and for what purpose. The essential component of privacy is control. If society or business is to preserve even a modicum of personal integrity, there has to be some control over use and access to the information contained in those giant data bases. Control is essential to optimum protection and use of information.

A second principle spinning out from the evolution of an information society is respect for the social context in which the information is created, used or communicated. To repeat: information is power. Those who teach the skills associated with the creation and use of information must inculcate respect for the society in which that power is used. Otherwise, you have the gamesmanship attitude of the "hackers" and "phone freaks" who delight in disrupting the lives and businesses that depend on that information. The "dark side" of the power can be countered only by teaching the moral and ethical limitations that are the internal "connectors" of the society, preserving order and personal respect. Therefore, if control of information is survival, then teaching the information operators the society's moral and ethical context is the essence of that control.

2. Technology is being matched with compensatory human

response, in order to amplify, rather than to overwhelm, human skills and needs. There is a need to maintain the connection between human touch and integrity. Indeed, as offices become more automated, employers have become concerned with the "work environment." They are trying to maintain a "human context" in order to motivate the people to increase market demand, a growing number of who operate the machines. Manufacturers are creating products that are touted for "ease of use" in addition to efficiency. It is clearly apparent that machines are being constructed to "augment" rather than replace people. The intent is to expand mind and motor strength and reach (human capability), while preserving spirit. So survival does not depend on fear (fighting the technology) but on adaptability acquiring the skills needed to operate and "live with" the new technology.

3.   Our society is part of a worldwide economic system in which a change to one remote country will affect the entire integrated global structure. Booming third world populations have strained the economies of developed countries because of the competition for resources. As those countries acquire more high technology, their "reach" will increase, putting even more stress on static resources. To survive, therefore, all peoples must use technology efficiently to increase food and energy supplies as well as to insure a "personal stake" for each individual in the globally integrated economy. Otherwise, the hackers of today

could become the terrorists of tommorrow, using the "dark side" of technology to assuage feelings of deprivation, anger and isolation.

4.   Long-term considerations have replaced the "tunnel vision" of the "now" (immediate gratification) generation. In the future, board meetings, quarterly reports, and production runs will be changing to the planned use of resources over the long term to maximize the impact of technology. The use of information to restructure the allocation of resources over the long-haul instead of the short-term is the "real" business impact of the new technology. The ability to expand "reach" by estimating capacity, needs and market demand over the long view has turned short-term business planning into strategic economic considerations. Both government and business are hiring experts like Mr. Mike Daniels to help evaluate the effect of events over the long-haul in order to understand impact on the global economic network. So control means using technology to understand the strategic effects of decision.

5.   There has been a rediscovery that small groupings can generate the entrepreneurial spirit that motivates innovation. "Small is beautiful!" This fact has been discovered by such giants as IBM, Digital Equipment Corporation and others who have spun off small, independent employee groupings (enterprises) to create new technology. Unhampered by corporate bureacracy, these

groupings are generating new products faster than would be possible within the larger, overwhelming business structure. Technology has emphasized individual achievement, expanded creative capacity and energized the entrepreneurial spirit. No better example exists of that trend than the high technology industry itself. New ideas are turned into advanced technology at a startling rate. Multimillion dollar businesses spring up-- virtually overnight--as small one-man shops grow into corporate monoliths on the sale of software or hardware products that give users a competitive edge. To prevail, technology demands constant innovation. The freedom to create, think, express and do are all essential to the new technology. Survival means encouraging innovation and growth through laws that recognize and stimulate the entrepreneurial spirit.

6.   Self-reliance has become the basis for accommodation with the new technology. As awareness grows that the new technology can amplify and extend the reach of human capability, the traditional values associated with individualism emerge to direct the application of innovation. Instead of technology being used to create universal dependence, it is being applied to individual opportunities, given new life to small businesses and cottage industries. Now, the individual no longer has to depend on a corporate giant to create job opportunities. By using technology, cash flow, communication, project turn-around, employee recruitment and overall management of resources can be

controlled by one person, as opposed to the ten people once needed to handle all those jobs. Result: the perception that only corporate giants have the resources to stimulate economic growth has changed in favor of individual initiative. With the aid of technology, the power of the nimble entrepreneur has been magnified to where the corporate giant must seek out the individual to acquire the innovation and skills needed to penetrate a market. Hence, the recent round of software company acquisitions by Fortune 500 companies who have found that the small organization has the power to perform effectively where the giant is too muscle-bound to respond. So, survival means recognizing individual opportunities created by the new technology's amplification of "reach." In essence, only fear limits potential. For those who are tired of the proverbial "rat-race", wake up. It doesn't have to be a "rat-race." Technology can amplify an individual's ability to compete, so that one need only creativity and persistance to turn a dream into reality.

7. Representative democracy is made obsolete by instaneous communication. The pressure for immediate knowledge about crucial issues has overwhelmed the slow, bureaucratic machinery of representative government. People cannot wait to determinethe status of an issue that affects the quality of life. Women's rights, environmental sensitivity, nuclear hazards, and avoidance of war are all issues that are of immediate concern,

337

and so are often decided more by the media than by the people's elected representatives--because the latter are unable to respond quickly. The new technology has unleashed the power of public opinion. Pressure can be generated almost immediately for issues of national concern. Small lobby groups can use technology to magnify their impact by motivating an overwhelming public outcry. Elected officials can be swamped by waves of constituant information on virtually any issue, reducing their ability to independently formulate positions. The portent for government is twofold: (a) that it is more difficult to hide bad decisions that impair the public interest; and (b) it is more difficult to rationally debate and decide one matter without the pressure of intense public scrutiny. So coping means that representative democracy will have to adapt and be more responsive than it has been to the pressures generated by technology. Already, some state governments are beginning to experiment with interactive communication, permitting constituants to vote directly on issues, or at least respond directly to electronic issue questionnaires. The latter will probably be the shape of representative democracy in the information age. Constituants will have the opportunity to instantaneously involve themselves in the decision-making process by electronic response/inquiry. The public demand for such instantaneous involvement will grow geometrically in all areas of government decision making, from the legislative to the executive until the shape of government has changed to accommodate those demands. The nature of those

338

changes and how they affect the quality of life are the real questions of survival. Will government be so democratized that momentary public pressure will control policy? If so, then survival will mean coping with a form of daily anarchy. The other scenario is that public opinion will be manipulated by government information (propaganda) so that pressure will be diffused and, indeed, ingored--permitting government to make decisions on its own, rather than in the public interest. Neither situation is particularly palatable. Accordingly, how can we maintain the benefit soft participatory democracy in an age of instantaneous communication without jeopardizing the liberties that have become the cornerstone of our society? This, obviously, is a difficult question. It can be answered only by a knowledgeable public willing to strike a balance between the undeniable integrity of Constitutional rights and the instantaneous exercise of those rights.

8.   Networks of people tied together by lines of communication are replacing hierarchal structures. No longer will the top-down theory be the basis for effective decision-making. Now, the electronic link between people forms a bond, unleashing creativity and movement, permitting a greater degree of interdependence. The facilitator has become the new leader. An example is the rise of small companies that have access to networks of experts who, on an independent contract basis, give those small companies tremendous economic potential. Networks

project power. By combining skills and creative powers, networks of people can, through interaction, resolve matters faster and more expeditiously than most corporate hierarchical structures. So coping means flexbility: a willingess to use technology in creating a network that permits broad interaction, magnifying the capability to resolve problems.

9.   Population has shifted toward the South and West, fueling a boom in economic growth that has outstripped the older cities of the North and East. Although older cities like New York will continue to be important centers of information and finance, most of the opportunity for new jobs associated with emerging high technology industry will gravitate toward the sunbelt.   This is because more flexibility exists in a new environment. It is often easier to get financing for development of new products in areas that have a relatively fresh and receptive climate, such as the Sunbelt, than in older, more industrialized areas burdened by complex hierarchical tax and finance structures.   Again, coping means that the economic climate has to nurture high technology by offering the means of quickly turning ideas into economic reality.   If the older (North/East) sections of the country desire to attract the opportunities associated with a fast-paced economic climate, the existing tax, property and finance structures will have to be modified to create greater individual flexbility.

340

10.   The information age has created a multi-option society. More types of consumer goods, such as cars, household items, clothing, etc., have appeared in the last five years than existed in the previous ten.   More job skills have been created at a faster rate than ever existed in the past--along with more opportunity for individual economic growth and intellectual development.   Growth is a function of options.   If your options are increasing, there is gain; if they are decreasing, there is loss.   High technology extends human potential, thereby increasing options.   So coping means using that increased potential to expand options, adding to the quality of life.

C.   A STRATEGIC VIEW

During an interview with Mr. John Norris Maquire, Chairman of the Board, President and Chief Executive Officer for Software AG Systems Group Inc., he expressed his own strategic concerns.   The following is a limited extrapolation of Mr. Maquire's thoughts and conclusions.

(a)   The software industry is global.   Vendors must have an international perspective to effectively market their products. The world is tied together by an increasingly sophisticated communications net that demands an integrated market view.   The industry, like Software AG, must take the long view to compete effectively by factoring international economic, social and

341

political considerations into an overall marketing perspective.

(b) Educational institutions have not created the skills needed to produce the type of innovative software technology marketed by Software AG. A gap exists between the needs of the industry and existing educational programs. Unless educational institutions forge a closer relationship with the software industry, that gap will widen, leaving graduates with a skills deficit that will have to be made up by the industry at a cost to its marketing resources.

(c) Protection of privacy is a function of end-use application. Those who buy and use the products have the responsibility to obey the laws and operate within the context of the society. All products, from soap to software, can be abused. It is the industry's function to create, and the user's to apply, within the bounds of propriety.

D. REFLECTIONS

Comprehension is the first step in coping with any problem, particularly one as diverse as the new technology's impact on society. The trends discussed in the chapter, as amplified by Mr. Maquire's sage perceptions, should provide a framework to help the reader understand and ultimately deal with the pressures generated by those changes. Untimately, it all boils down to how the individual can cope with a society in the throes of metamorphosis. Perhaps the answer is really knowing who you are, understanding personal needs, and accepting the technology as a means of extending each. Copying is reaching: using the tools of technology to reshape, reform, and ultimately recreate an an environment that supports the diverse levels of potential.